BETWEEN MARRIAGE
AND DIVORCE
A Woman's Diary

BETWEEN MARRIAGE AND DIVORCE
A Woman's Diary

by Susan Braudy

WILLIAM MORROW AND COMPANY, INC.
NEW YORK   1975

Printed in the United States of America.

1 2 3 4 5 79 78 77 76 75

Library of Congress Cataloging in Publication Data

Braudy, Susan.
  Between marriage and divorce.

  1. Braudy, Susan. 2. Wives—Biography. 3. Divorcees—Biography. 4. Women—Sexual behavior. I. Title.
HQ1413.B7A33   301.42′7′0924   75-16468
ISBN 0-688-02960-4

DESIGN: HELEN ROBERTS

This book is nonfiction, based on my diaries and memories. I have changed the names of a few of the characters. Some of the reactions I write about were overheated, but they represent my responses at the time.

I tell this story, my story, because its outline and emotional content are common ones. In the ordinariness of my own private feelings, I hope other women can see their own. We are unsurprisingly not alone.

Sometimes I think it is not that I and a growing number of women and men have failed at marriage, but that the institution of marriage has failed us. Margaret Mead has said most cultures honor concepts which people publicly uphold but privately and shamefully fail to live up to. She suggests marriage is such a concept.

I dedicate the book to my brother Leonard Orr and to Suzanne Levine. I'd like to thank Sophy Burnam, Mary Thom, Harvey Shapiro, Mary Peacock, Lynn Young, Brian DePalma, Ross Wetzsteon, Nina Finkelstein, and Jackie Farber for their friendship and help.

S.B.

We struggle and suffer to reconquer
our solitude.
　　　　　　—ALBERT CAMUS, *Carnets*

The future always looks good in the golden land
because no one remembers the past.
　　—JOAN DIDION, *Slouching Toward Bethlehem*

At lucky moments we seem on the brink
Of really saying what we think we think,
But even then an honest eye should wink.
　　　　　　　　　—W. H. AUDEN

AUGUST

The country and western concert is blaring at the outdoor theater in Saratoga Springs. But Jim St. Clare, the Cajun singer, hasn't arrived.

Backstage is tawdry. As they comb their pompadours and ducktail hairdos, the country musicians look repulsive and glamorous. Their buttocks squeezed into pink dungarees, they swagger around in matching pink cowboy boots. " 'Tain't likely he'll show atall," muses one musician. "He's weird." His laugh is slow and phlegmy, like a cigarette cough.

Last summer a national audience saw Jim St. Clare play the violin and sing on the "Tonight Show." Whooping and leaping and scratching at his electric fiddle, he was a frenzied demon, thrusting his pelvis and staring into the camera with his dark, sad, deep-set eyes.

At the outdoor theater, St. Clare arrives four hours late. Dressed in an emerald-green tight velvet suit, he is the only longhair backstage. He flips his guitar over a bright velvet shoulder and paces the backstage hallways quietly singing about the Mississippi River, oblivious to the loudspeaker blasting out the first acts on stage. Listening to St. Clare sing is a way to learn about the different people who share America.

St. Clare turns to find a reporter behind him in the hall-

way. "Hold m'hand honey. Please, it makes me less nervous."
Three grabs and finally her hand is holding his wrist and vi-
brating near the neck of his guitar while they pace together.
After opening several doors, he chooses a dressing room with
yellow seats. He likes yellow. Catching sight of himself in the
mirror, he sees a drop of blood on his cheek. "Jesus," he moans
without straining his low, easy voice, "I wanted to look per-
fect, just perfect. This-here ain't no place for a country boy."

Suddenly he explodes. The reporter is making him ner-
vous because she's so nervous after having waited for him for
five hours. He grabs her hand again and puts it inside his
narrow velvet lapel. "Don't you be nervous now. Here, honey,
feel m'heart. We're all human. . . ."

That's the way my article for the *Village Voice* began.
But I could sense it was getting too personal, that in order to
be honest, I had to say much more. I realized how much
journalism had been my crutch. I wrote impersonally about
other people because I was afraid to look too closely at myself.
So I decided to finish writing my article about Jim St. Clare
later. Tonight, I decided, I'll start writing in my journal about
what really happened when I went to interview him.

It was that first touching Jim St. Clare's chest and feeling
the bumping inside. It's not easy for me to touch people. His
shirt was silk and I felt the sweat beginning under it. He
smelled a lot of violets and I saw the dried hairspray like a
spider's web on his long, shiny black hair. Up close his eyes
looked more melancholic because of the worry lines in the
corners. His mouth looked tighter and crueler. The tiny dots
of his dark heavy beard made him look a little seedier than
he looked from across the room or on stage.

The other musicians had been eyeing me furtively all
day. Their faces were pouchy from whiskey, their eyes nar-
rowed by lost fantasies of greed. I knew if these guys didn't
stink of perfume they'd smell like the ash trays and sweaty

upholstery of the bus they lived in. One man lit a match on
the sole of his pink boot and pretended I wasn't there, as he
said, "That gal with the schoolteacher manners and the long
legs sure-as-shootin' has it for ol' Jim. She's been hangin'
around for him all the day long. He'll get into that today, or
maybe that's somethin' poor ol' Jim can't do himself anymore
now that he pops all them city pills and goes on the teevee all
the time."

They didn't believe I was a reporter, even though I'd
made notes all day about the smells of the pines and their
cowboy clothes. Several of them did advise me to go home.
That he'd never come. But I'd called and called St. Clare's
bored New York agent for a month, demanding his daily
county fair and nightclub schedule in small towns in Okla-
homa, Florida, and finally in New York. After I'd seen him
last spring on the "Johnny Cash Show," I had to write about
him and his music. He was a potential pop star, singing in his
native Cajun tradition.

I didn't sleep much the night before I went to Saratoga
Springs. I love reporting, but the prospect still scares me—
even though I've been doing it for several years. People say
reporters must be aggressive. I'm more tenacious. Once I begin,
I cover the story for days and days. I keep observing and
writing notes. I also write and rewrite my pieces over and
over. When I'm reporting, I worry that I'll fall and twist my
ankle far from home where nobody will help me. I worry that
I'll leave my notebooks in a cab or a diner. I've done that
twice. I guess I am scared that I can't manage without my
husband.

When St. Clare arrived I forgot I was afraid. I didn't
even care what I looked like to the other performers. I lost
my overly proper, self-watching self. I told myself it was because I was a reporter and supposed to observe him, that I
allowed him to place my arm in the tight green velvet sweati-
ness between his elbow and his side, and then I obediently

paced the floor with him while he played his guitar. I forgot
who I was. My own voice sounded clipped, nasal and un-
musical, while he sounded like a 45 record playing at 33,
hypnotic.

"Honey, don't you worry about afterwards. We'll go back
to my motel. I'll get out of mah work clothes, and we'll order
us up a big dinner. And I'll tell you everything about mah
life. Happiness and sadness are part of the same thing, hon.
They both make me cry. And you'll tell me everything about
you. I'm gonna be real big. Johnny Cash offered me six spots
and the opening for next month. I'm gonna get me a movie
star career. Yes sir, things have sure been happening to me
that I always knew would come about ever since I was a-fishing
them swamps with mah daddy."

When he tells about his father, his voice quivers and he
stops a beat or two for dramatic effect. I suspect the story
is partly a hype, but I also know he believes it himself, so I
was excited to hear the words I'd read in newspaper articles.
It meant I'd done my research in the clipping files of *The New
York Times* well. I was in control to the extent that I knew a
lot more about him than he suspected. "He shot himself in
the head, honey, on that-there houseboat he was floating on.
I found his body myself. I was six, and had to shoo away the
chickens. They were pecking up his brains. I never knew why
mah daddy did what he did, but I come to terms with it, yes sir.
He fought his fight and I'll fight mine."

Then the loudspeaker blared his name—"Jim St. Clare,
Jim St. Clare"—and he pulled his guitar strap over his shoulder
and he was gone. So I walked out the stage door and into the
audience. On stage he was jumping, fiddling, and yodeling,
but there was a disappointing buzz of talk coming from the
audience. Once he tried to joke about how his mother had
bought her first pair of store teeth before she came to visit
him in Hollywood, but the audience only giggled nervously.
I took notes and watched the act. I loved it. He's a good

fiddler and he was singing his heart out, but the applause was only casual as he wrapped up the set.

When I walked backstage, I was afraid I'd lost him. Then I saw the green velvet suit and the black hair. He caught my eye and nodded. As I pushed through the crowd of country musicians, I hoped he would let me ask him the questions I'd been scribbling in my notebook since yesterday. Access is everything. The first rule of reporting is to get people to trust you enough to admit you into their world. I stood by his side for a minute while he whispered into the ear of a tiny blond woman dressed in a green tulle ballerina skirt. "Oh yes, hon?" He twisted his head around to me, keeping his arm on her shoulders. "Let's go. Grab that fiddle case, now." I walked behind him clutching the violin and my notebooks to my chest. In the motel lobby I stopped. I'd checked into this motel too and I was exhausted and scared to go to his room. "Aah, I'll go to my room for a while," I suggested.

"Now, hon," his voice was irritable, "you want to come up or not? I haven't eaten yet. Have you?" "No," I shook my head no. In fact I hadn't eaten since nine that morning. "Well then, just come up. I'll change mah duds, and order up some club sandwiches, and we can talk and talk. Don't be running off like that. It makes me nervous. You don't want to make me nervous, now." I needed to be alone. But I'd waited so long. One look at his angry face and I knew I had to follow him, or risk losing the chance to interview him. Elusive subjects are impossible. I had interviewed people in hotel rooms a few times before. Nothing could go wrong.

Up in his room he disappeared to take a shower, and I sat there like the faculty wife and working reporter that I am, taking notes about the messy motel room littered with guitar strings, crusts of old club sandwiches, rumpled mounds of silk and velvet clothing, and empty Scotch bottles. Then he emerged in a gray silk jumpsuit with a seam split on the side that showed he was wearing no underwear.

He ordered us two turkey club sandwiches and politely asked if he could sit next to me on the bed. I said, formally, "Please don't."

While I wrote, he answered my questions, plucked his guitar, and crooned a New Orleans patois to himself. Something was annoying him. After an hour, he leaned across my lap and tilted my chin up while he asked sadly, "Don't you like me?" I nodded and twisted my head away, reaching nervously for the glass of Chivas Regal he'd poured for me. "Yes, I like your work, that's why I came this distance to write the piece." Then I knew I should leave, so after about ten minutes I smiled broadly and said, "Enough for tonight. We should get some sleep." He was silent. Then he smiled. "No, let me tell you about the time mah daddy . . ." And so it went. And then he asked again if he could sit closer by me on the bed, and he filled my glass with Chivas Regal. Soon he was trying to show me some guitar fingerings, sitting close and pushing my fingers around on the neck of the guitar. He was patting the ends of my hair saying it was "purty, purty," and I liked to feel him touching me, and soon it was 4:00 A.M. and I was drunker than I'd ever been. And I also knew I could leave, because I'd got a better interview from him than any I'd seen.

I didn't mean to sleep with him. I don't know. No man had ever sung and sighed at me like that. Or if they had, it had happened to an adolescent me too long ago. By sunrise, I was still pretending I was the relentlessly decent woman scribbling a lyric in my notebook he'd crooned to me and I was shaking my head, no. "No, no. Well, I don't want you to kiss me on the cheek, or stroke my arm—it tickles my whole body. No, I don't want to just go to sleep in the other single bed. No, I don't want you to hug me like that." I was beginning to forget why, why this man couldn't hug me. I felt like a teen-ager in a *True Romance* story unable or unwilling to figure out what I was doing. I remembered the backstage musicians and felt irritable because they seemed to know more about me and Jim than I knew. But I liked him and he moved me with his melancholy and his need to make me like him. Then I'd remember to say, "Don't kiss me and sigh because you think I'm touching when I tell you about my happy marriage to a young professor sleeping without me in New York." My husband must never know I was so exhausted that I just crawled under the covers of the other single bed and tried to go to sleep. We didn't sleep.

Then I wanted to cry I was so happy. I forgot that a man touching me could feel so amazing. Sex with a new man is something I never expected again in my life. I must not think of my husband. I must not feel guilty. It's so easy with this weird stranger. I'm feeling this for me. Paul is not here. Usually a reporter and a strange subject fake an instant intimacy to get a good interview. This interview is passing into real life.

My husband—rational, dutiful, devoted—would never stay up with me past 2:00 A.M., not even when I begged him to while we were courting ten years ago. I remember when we were in our late teens, he sang a folk song softly at a party, plucking on an untuned guitar and looking at me out of the corner of his eye to see if I was listening. But as adults, we work, he helps me schedule, we don't show off to each other, we don't make disorder, we don't stay up late, we don't commit adultery, we don't make demands, we never get drunk, and we wouldn't remember if we ever made love with groans and sweet talk. Jim says he has a master's degree in mathematics. I don't believe him. He says he's never seen the inside of a subway. I believe him. And writing this, I wonder about the other women who have believed him when he says, "I need you, honey. Don't be doin' me like that honey. Say yes. You lo-uve it like I do, don't you, honey?"

August 7: Afternoon

Waking alone in that motel room, I called Paul collect in New York. I told him I was staying up in Saratoga Springs till tonight, so I wouldn't see him before he left for his seminar in California. He sounded the same. I did too. "That's okay honey, just get a good story," he said, forever the patient adult. It's probably better, I told myself as I hung up the telephone, because if I were in New York to say good-bye to him, I'd feel awful and left-behind. But even after having sex with somebody else, I feel hurt Paul isn't more unhappy that we're apart. Amazing.

Sometimes when Paul rushes into the bedroom to kiss me loudly on the lips in the early morning and bounds out the door to go to class, I am seized with a cramp of rejection. I'm afraid he prefers whatever is outside the door to me. And I suffer. Sometimes if he says good-bye on the telephone too eagerly or before I'm ready, I get the same pain. To protect myself from this bereft feeling, I often rush to hang up the telephone first, or as now—I'm not returning to New York so he can leave me. It's just as well that I'm here in Saratoga Springs, I tell myself, wiping Paul from my mind as I turn from the red telephone on the formica night table and the open Scotch bottles to stare at the three red velvet suits hanging on a corner rack next to the pile of fiddle and guitar cases.

August 7: Evening

Several hours later I dashed through the clusters of nighttime travelers at the Albany airport behind Jim in his tight red velvet suit and a ruffled black transparent shirt. Every once in a while I found myself talking to myself—silently moving my lips. "This is incredible," I would mouth. This long-haired person whose narrow back was covered in fire-engine red silk, where does he get the right to take my arm and push me past the gawking travelers? My God, what have I done? "Honey, you write a good story now." He pushed his face close to mine so that our noses bumped. I ducked my head. "Let me get your ticket home," he ordered. I shook my head no, as he shouted, "Hey," and motioned imperiously to his road manager bent double under a load of amplifiers, guitars, and suitcases.

Jim lowered his voice to whisper, his rumbly voice tickling my ear. "You had a good time last night?" His words hinted at a question as though he was beginning an explanation to a stupid child. "Yes," I answered breathlessly, feeling a wash of physical sensations. And I ruefully remembered the love comics I'd read as a teen-ager whose heroines would clasp their hands and ask, "Does he *thrill* when he thinks of *our night?*" "Well, didja?" and here his voice became tighter and softer, slightly ominous. "Honey child, didja have your best time?" "Yes." I was still breathless, hoping we were talking silly good lover talk. "Well," and here he sighed elaborately, shaking his head gently from side to side, "didja ever stop and wonder whether I had mah best time?" I jerked my head around to stare at his lowered eyelids and disapproving mouth.

"Well, umm, didn't you?" I began. I felt upset, even though I was about to get on a plane and go hundreds of miles away from this strange man. "No Ma'am, I didn't." "Well, umm," and now I felt as though I was starting to fall down in a dream. He actually didn't feel as wonderful as I had just politely claimed I did about this. "Well, umm," and I thought of six ways of phrasing the question, all of them wrong and unsubtle. "I mean, what didn't I, I mean, what was wrong?" "Honey, I was so tired from sweet-talking you and worrying about you that I didn't have mah release." He stared at me reprovingly, proud, I couldn't help observing, of his euphemism. "And you nevah noticed atall?" He sighed and then waved grandly to an old Black man wearing a red cap and pushing a wire baggage cart. "Pappy, you too northern and uppity to help us out here with some things?"

Relieved that our sex talk was finished, I was still conscious enough to be horrified by this bad joke. I watched the porter's face for signs of anger. But he laughed, ducked his head, and pulled his cap off to slide it back on pretending to smooth his tightly frizzed hair. "Yassuh, yassuh," he kept saying as he pushed the wardrobe bags and instrument cases into the ticket line behind a woman in a red maternity dress. I walked into another line for the New York airplane to buy my ticket, happy to leave Jim and his sexual questions behind.

August 7: Midnight

Home alone. I'm in a daze. I can't unpack my airflight bag. I keep wandering the six rooms of my Central Park West apartment playing Jim's record over and over. First I find my feet pacing the border of the Oriental rug in the hallway, then I'm in Paul's study, my eyes running over the titles of his books stacked on white bookshelves. Why haven't I read any of these seventeenth-century English history studies he specializes in? Maybe because they are his turf. He has them all figured out. I think about how he grunts while he's reading a book and how he gets that self-satisfied sideways smile on his face when someone tells him he looks like Marlon Brando. I tell him he barely does, but other people have mentioned it to both of us over the years.

This is a rare separation for us. I close my eyes and picture his slanty Cossack blue eyes that dart from side to side when he starts to get a new idea. Sometimes when I kiss his face over and over, his eyelids half close and his full mouth goes soft. When I see him in a crowd walking toward me, limping slightly, his shoulders back, his swimmer's chest forward, I think, *my husband.*

What's he doing right now? Who's he talking to in California?

August 9

This afternoon I called Judith and told her I had to see her. I was conscious of the drama I was creating. I can't decide if I should be embarrassed about being so self-indulgent lately. She arrived an hour later to kiss me on the cheek and then stare at me when she thought I wouldn't notice. "Are you all right?" She asked gently.

Judith Roberts seems to love me in a very uncritical way. At college, when our best mutual friend in the dormitory had a nervous breakdown, we'd take the Greyhound bus from Philadelphia to New York to visit her. Though we had barely spoken before these trips, we got in the habit on those long busrides of comforting each other and trying to explain away each other's guilty feelings toward our sick friend. We shared mutual bouts of nervous indigestion, aggravated by the lurching old buses. Later, Judith visited me a few times in New Haven when she was studying for her Ph.D. in clinical psychology and living in New York on the lower East Side with a jazz drummer and I was a Yale faculty wife. For each of us, it was an exciting excursion into another life-style. We marveled that we had so much in common.

We're both a little taller than 5'9", and had to suffer

adolescent gawkiness. We still feel shy and self-effacing, as though we have to emotionally negate the impact of our size. Judith, however, has a model's face, planed like a Greek statue. At college she had short, flyaway hair, embarrassed limbs, and a librarian's countenance behind horn-rimmed glasses. Once she came to New York though, she seemed to bloom. Now she wears tight denim pants and a bandana tied at the back of her neck under her waist-length hair. She's had many post-college affairs, and recently told me about a six-course seafood meal that turned into a sex orgy where her host decided to punish his best friend by not inviting him. The best friend kept calling on the telephone and begging to be allowed to come and watch.

Before I started being a New York reporter two years ago, Judith was my only friend who lived this sort of life. It is only through her stories and my reporting assignments from *New York* magazine and *The New York Times Magazine* that I know people like Jim St. Clare. In Philadelphia where I grew up, my parents never discussed alternatives to their monogamous marriage except in elliptical anger or jokes. Once I picked up the telephone and heard my father tell my mother he was staying overnight in Baltimore where he was attending a conference. I was frightened for her, wondering from the sighing sounds in her voice and the appeasing note to his if she felt he was being disloyal to her in a way she was forced to put up with as a wife. In New Haven, Paul and I had been part of a group of young academic couples, all committed, it seemed to me, to living out my parents' ideals. Paul is the only man I ever slept with until this week.

I didn't want to make my sexual confession to Judith inside my house, my husband's house. So I put on my sweater and we walked silently into the dusty greenery of Central Park. It was six o'clock, and the sideburned psychiatrists who live nearby were walking their Irish Setters on winding paths. A few kids were walking in the playground, and a jogger almost knocked Judith over because we stopped to admire the intense greens of the grass and the trees in the gray evening light.

As we fell back into step, I told her, "Well, I slept with someone." She hit my arm and said, "Oh, you're too much," when I told her about staying up all night and taking notes on what was turning into a sexual seduction. I explained to Judith, "Listen, reporters are hit with mental seductions all the time. When you interview somebody, they drive themselves crazy trying to get you to love them so you'll write them up well. I never felt susceptible to a sexual pass before. It's part of the subtext of the game female and male reporters learn to play. Meanwhile, they're trying to disarm the celebrity to get the real dope."

But I had to find out Judith's ideas about what had happened. "Tell me, have I done something disgusting?" I demanded. "Yes," I thought, as she muttered, "I don't know." Adultery, my mind raced through her silence—the unplanned act of adultery. I never thought it would happen to me. Then I asked her, "Am I supposed to call him on the phone? Will we see each other again? What is he thinking? And I haven't ruined my thing with Paul? What do you think?" Judith sighed.

"Let's walk over to Broadway for a cup of coffee," I suggested. "It's too dark to stay in the park." It was a weird note of propriety, but we both knew that we could not go back to my house to have this discussion. "Did you enjoy it?" she asked after five minutes of walking. "Yes," I answered. But I certainly hadn't enjoyed the worrying and calling Paul and Jim's reproachful remarks. But I enjoyed looking into his eyes, getting to know him, having the sex, and having an adventure of my own.

In the coffee shop we faced each other. "Susan, I can't tell you what it means." I felt a new respect from her, perhaps part of the reason I had chosen to ask her for help. "It means what you want it to mean," she continued. "What *I* want it to mean or what *Jim* wants it to mean?" I asked. "How will

I know what he wants if we don't talk about it?" Then I felt fatuous talking to Judith in romantic clichés. But I have no perspective, no vocabulary, no real sense of what has just happened to me.

"If you two don't talk about it, then you'll have decided something," she replied. I lowered my chin weakly on my folded hands, wondering if Judith now thought of me as more sophisticated or more sneaky.

I asked again, "Should I call him?" "I can't answer you," she whispered. "Well," I asked boldly, "what has it meant to you when you've slept with guys?" She stopped sipping her coffee and stared at me over the top of her wire-rimmed glasses. "It's meant everything or nothing, depending on what we wanted it to mean."

August 10: Noon

Everything and nothing. I feel stupid. I must be an ostrich. But I never worried before about what sex could mean. When Paul and I slept together at age nineteen back in 1960, it was a simpler era; we were silently pledging a betrothal. After we did the awkward act in his parents' bedroom one summer Sunday afternoon, he slipped a paper cigar band on my ring finger. We both knew the gesture was of a higher order than the one he'd made the day before when, after shaving off his beard, he had shaved my initials in the hair on his thigh.

August 10: Night

3:00 A.M. This is the second time tonight I've awakened in an empty king-sized bed, and at first, in the dark, I thought

I was still in that motel room. Maybe the trucks rumbling down the street twelve floors below woke me up. Paul and I are not separated much. I am the one who goes away, lately anyway, for reporting assignments. I don't think I've slept alone at home for years. Without another person, without Paul breathing deeply in sleep or making noises in another part of the house, I don't feel alive.

Writing about it helps. It gives me the illusion that I am in control. With the little desk lamp on, I can type without shocking my eyes with bright light. I can't stay in my rumpled bed. Empty, it feels like a reproach. It is my marital bed and I have violated it. Talking about it with Judith was an attempt to get absolution.

I've broken the major promise I've made in my adult life. I remember a 4:00 A.M. session one night in college with a handsome pre-divinity student who explained Kierkegaard's existentialism to me, while he drank four double Scotches. "You particularize yourself," he explained, rubbing his eyes with long fingers while I wished he would focus his intensity on me. "Every time you choose to eat roast beef or break your promise, you lock out other choices, and you've become the sort of person who eats roast beef or breaks promises. You are your history."

August 11

Paul didn't call tonight. I paced into his study and switched on the light to consult his typewriter, silent and secretive. The house feels strange without the fierce clatter of his two-fingered typing. But maybe something has happened to him out there. Anyway, if I can have sex with someone else, why can't he? Just the thought makes my stomach hurt. I feel a quick flash of anger and then fear that I have no right to feel possessive after what I've done. I am driving myself crazy with these thoughts. I called Jim's house in Nashville today and let it ring fourteen times before I hung up. There's nothing I have to say to him, nothing, I kept telling myself, or him to me. I dialed again just to make sure he wasn't home.

But I really want Paul home. I want to feel that nothing has changed. I never thought about whether the idea of marriage contains the idea of adultery. I don't know. There are a lot of things I haven't thought about. I keep telling myself that everything will be all right, but I feel more tense.

August 12

3:00 A.M. It's midnight in California, so I just stopped typing and called Paul again. "Oh hi, honey, I haven't had a chance to call," he said, sounding bored. I knew I was hiding my panic, but I wondered if he'd noticed it anyway, since things are so regularized, so ritualized between us.

"I'm okay, well, not really, I mean I can't sleep, I think I'm a little out of it because I feel so alone," I stumbled. "Well, as long as you're writing," he said. "Yes," I answered, "I'm working on the piece about the country singer." All I've been writing is this diary, after the first few paragraphs of my article. "Well, I wish you were here to help me."

But this wasn't the first time I'd lied to Paul. Suddenly I remembered the television show host in Detroit who took me drinking after I spoke on an educational television talk show and then kissed me good-night about six times at the door of my hotel. "You don't know what you're missing out on," he kept whispering. I was very drunk and kissing him made my legs feel weak. But I kept thinking about Paul and how I didn't want to have to contemplate equity in this matter.

So I went to sleep. Kisses don't count, I remember saying out loud, still high on them as I pulled my clothes off in the darkness of that hotel room and went to sleep alone. But I never told Paul about the kissing.

"I'll help you when I get back, honey," Paul was saying. "I'll look at your article in a week. Peter and Joanne send their love. Now try to get some sleep."

I need to tell him what I've done, I thought. If I tell him when he returns, will he scream and throw books at me and then walk out? Or would he sit down to cry and we'd both know that I couldn't put my arms around his shoulders to comfort him, because I was the cause of his pain. Or would he simply decide that he would have sex with others, a thought that again terrorized me. If he were to forgive me, that would take a lot of the pressure and guilt off me. But that is selfish. He shouldn't suffer because I've done this. I have to bear the guilt myself.

My panic does not subside. I feel sorry for us. I want to believe a marriage can survive this kind of thing. Of course it can, because I'll make sure it does.

August 13: Morning

Yesterday my psychiatrist—who I sometimes think feels I'm a big baby—laughed gleefully when I got to the middle of telling the Jim St. Clare story, and said, "Get to the point, you fucked with him, right, and now you think you're going to die of it." We agreed I wouldn't tell Paul, because it wasn't fair to make him feel bad. I first started seeing her a year ago because I had a writer's block. She seemed a freakish addition to my life. I refused to talk with her about Paul because I thought it was telling secrets. But since I've started doing things I can't tell Paul about, I need her more and more. She's a great believer in doing things you're afraid to do—and becoming a stronger person because the actions become easier and easier. "You'll be nicer to Paul now," she comforted me yesterday, pushing some stray gray hairs back into her chignon, "because you see that you don't have to be so dependent on him."

August 15: Evening

"I don't want to know about the fluctuations in Paul's love for me. I want to assume a loving, forgiving, constant feeling coming from him."

My shrink interrupted: "You don't allow him to have feelings the way you do." A scary idea. Yet I know I'm scared to hear about the women Paul is physically attracted to, let alone those he could love. In fact, most of the time I refuse to admit he could be attracted to anyone else. Why am I so easily betrayed?

Sometimes in the early years of our marriage, when he and I went to parties, I'd watch his eyes as he talked to different women. If he smiled very happily or began to lean close to someone, my stomach would tighten with envy and tension. How could he enjoy someone more than he enjoys me, I'd ask myself, conscious that my thoughts were senseless and were not making me happy. But they wouldn't go away. But of course why shouldn't he enjoy that woman more than me? My stomach would tense with rage.

Often after the party, I'd sulk and he'd first try to talk casually to me and then I'd hear the self-pity and anger in *his* voice, and he'd say, "What's the matter with you?" I'd refuse to say why I was miserable—out of pride, I'd tell myself. My hurt feelings were a weakness that must be hidden.

My shrink says I am wrong. She says they could have been revealed to Paul as a positive appeal for love or reassurance: for instance, "I love you, dear, and I know you love me and are good to me, but some feeling of unworthiness made me sad at the party. I got hurt because you spent so much time joking with that beautiful graduate student. It's ridiculous, but I felt like you'd given away something of mine when you called her dear in the silly falsetto you use when we're alone."

Instead of some tender explanation, I made myself a Gary Cooper. My rule: never admit weakness or fear. It hurts even now to say, "Paul, I love you so much I worry that someone else could make you happier."

August 17

When I called Paul in California last night, Joanne answered the telephone and told me breathlessly that she, Paul, and Peter had just gone swimming nude on a nearby beach. Stop it, stop it, I kept telling myself as I grew angrier. "Oh it was great, you should've been here. We all got suntans in new places." She giggled. "Paul loved swimming without clothes. Peter kept chasing him and flicking towels at him."

When Paul got to the phone, I pictured his body as in the private times when I alone saw it, after he'd taken a shower, his dark curls matted down to his head, at night before he slipped on his pajamas, and after we'd made love as he lay with his head on my shoulder, one hand stroking my hair.

"How are you, honey?" he asked cheerfully. The static of telephone wires across the continent made his voice sound husky. "Well," and then I was silent, uncertain whether the anger was coming from a sane or just place. "Well, I guess I feel lonely and panicky," I said in a rush, hedging my reactions.

As I spoke into the telephone, I wondered how Paul could really be so far away from me anyway. We were a duo, locked by mutual love and need into the same living space and rules for living. Now he was thousands of miles away and had been cavorting on the beach naked. Another woman saw his genitals, and the tight muscles where his upper legs meet his buttocks. I felt a sharp ache behind my eyes. Was it wrong to expect him to be the way I wanted him to be?

"Don't feel lonely. Call up Judith. And I'll be home soon." He sounded pressured and distant as we hung up the telephone.

Well, would you rather he came running home to hold your hand? asked a cold voice in my head. And the cold voice continued, Sweetheart, you need total devotion because maybe you never had it as a kid. It's a quick thought I've been through many times when Paul disappointed me by the secret standards I apply to measure his love. Once after we fought and fought because I didn't want to go to a faculty party, he stomped out of the room. If he really loved me, he wouldn't make these demands, I told myself sullenly. I held my breath until he walked resolutely back into the room and handed me a new book and then I felt the relief—he does love me.

August 19

Admit, admit I am scared to find out what I would learn about Paul if I looked too closely. I might suddenly discover one emotional fact that might prove he didn't love me, that I didn't love him, or that our whole relationship was a misunderstanding. We complain about friends, report on good movies or books, but we rarely talk about each other. I hope we haven't made a pact not to look at the details of our life together too closely.

I avoid asking Paul about the nude swimming episode. Did he get an erection? Was he afraid that he might? Was he overwhelmed at the sight of a nude woman—other than me? Did he ever think he was going to see another woman's body nude in his lifetime of marriage? I don't want to know about his having erections when he's not with me. He always refuses to tell me anything about women he slept with before we started seeing each other, even though I beg him. Sometimes I feel we should know each other's pasts—that our knowing about these people negates their importance. I guess Paul believes our romance needs secrecy. I've wanted to tell him about my first boyfriend, Noel, many times, but I've always stopped. It's odd, our lack of interest in our own sexual pasts when we find other people's so interesting, even threatening.

August 27

Last night he came back from his three weeks in California, suntanned and silent, and I stayed up until 3:00 A.M., asking, "What was it like? Why did you do it?" He was angry at first, and refused to answer me, punching his pillow, turning over and over, and finally sitting up against the gold headboard, his arms folded across his chest. Sometimes I think these fights I provoke are one of our few precious ways of being intimate. I wish I had learned other ways—but it's so hard for me to ask directly for reassurance.

"Okay, okay, I'll tell you what it was like." Paul shrugged, his shoulders hunched and tired. I was exhausted too, and crying. I guess I was wishing I could tell him about Jim. And I was scared. If it was so easy for me, maybe he had slipped into a sexual scene too. He crossed his arms tighter, his lower lip jutting out with exasperation. "It was very childlike, I guess. After the first couple of seconds wondering if you were going to, you didn't feel sexy at all." I sat up and turned my back to him, clasping my knees with my arms. I'd stopped crying. He was patting my back. "Oh, you know Peter, he flicked his towel at me a lot and acted like a locker-room jock. But the great thing was how free you feel, I mean close to the sand and the water in a way I never felt with trunks and a jockstrap on. I loved looking at the bodies against the white sand."

As he whispered, I made little noises of assent. I treasure the few times I've heard him describe his feelings. On the other hand, I am bored when he lectures me about what happened to the laws of England when they'd cut a king's head off.

So, tonight with the first feeling of empathy, my anger disappeared. Then I was guilt-stricken that I had kept him up late on his first night back. "Let's go to sleep," I whispered. "I feel better, and you have to teach tomorrow afternoon. I feel weird, but I understand a lot of things better now." I thought, well our world has been altered, Paul and I have both taken steps outside our agreed system of actions. But now he was back in bed with me, a familiar warm body silently drifting into sleep. Before I fell asleep, I had one more twinge. "How did Joanne act on the beach?" I asked. But he was asleep, his breathing regular and deep.

BACKGROUND

Back in 1957 when I was in high school, my first boy-friend Noel was usually away at college. But when he'd drive home for a random weekend or spring vacation, we'd devote hours to giggles and passion. We would squirm enthusiastically half in and half out of our clothes inside his family's car that he parked a few feet from my front lawn. We'd stop breathlessly only when headlight beams penetrated our windows as other cars pulled under the sycamore trees and turned off their motors in front of the small dark houses.

Finally, at about midnight, I'd stumble up the steps and into my parents' home, my body so sensualized that a shower was a continued delight. I usually grinned a few times to myself remembering our jokes or physical contortions before I fell asleep. I had no thought that our fun could ever end.

A year earlier Noel and I had argued for weeks about whether he could touch my breasts. One night because he seemed so sincere, I nodded yes, even though I knew my parents would think I was dirty and immoral. I was curious, too. He reverently put his palm on my chest while we were sitting in his car; and I got a lump in my throat, although I felt nothing particularly sensual. He gulped and whispered, "It's the first time, Susan. I've never done this before." His words were redundant. I knew how he felt. And it suddenly seemed right. All my reasons—the disgusted looks from my mother when she discussed my friends who might be necking and carrying on with men, my dread that we might forget ourselves, "go all the way," and end up with me pregnant— these seemed pointless now. "I love you," he'd whispered in his hoarsest voice.

One night I wobbled into my house and my mother was standing in the dark living room wearing her clean, faded flannel pajamas and smelling faintly of Ivory soap. "Oh hi," I said casually, hoping that Noel's car clock hadn't stopped, and conscious that she was an abrupt and unpleasant person to encounter moments after I had been writhing around in the car. "What were you doing out there?" she whispered, her voice shaking. "Nothing," I said too loudly. "Well, suppose your father had seen you out there in the car for hours, what do you think he'd say?"

In our home she was the judicious, objective one, he was the flamboyant, temperamental child. But if she ever gave him permission to overreact, he'd fly into a rage, heady with her approval. On subtle cue from my mother, he'd take his belt to me or my sister or my brother or throw a tantrum in front of my friends about cigarette smoking in the house. She was quiet, intellectual, fair, and depressed because she was the only person acting like an adult in the household. Why do we now dislike each other so much on the surface of our lives, when I feel so much for her?

But that night she stood there trembling in her flannel pajamas and bare feet, out of control for maybe the third time in our life together. "Well, I know what you were doing out there until all hours." Her voice was unsteady, and hard to control while she limited herself to whispering. "You were necking."

Her contempt was too much for me. "Yeah?"

My lack of abjectness was too much for her. The next

thing I felt was a ringing slap on my cheek and across my nose, a shock because in the dark I had no way to see it coming. So I rushed upstairs to my room and cried and cried to myself without turning on my light. I felt guilty for provoking her. I hated her for hating me, and even hated my friend for giving me the pleasure that caused my mother to punish me.

Paul at seventeen

Paul was an urban Jewish teen-ager's version of a dreamboat. He told me the night we met that his I.Q. was above 160, and he told me he was probably a "pre-potent sire." "A man whose genes are so filled with genius that he will sire a dynasty of brilliant minds like the Huxleys." I hated him for bragging. On the other hand, I wanted to marry him. We would sire geniuses and argue brilliantly for the rest of our lives. We were listening to Bach at a friend's house and admiring an elementary computer that the friend had built. I had already heard about Paul from a colleague of my mother's who taught him advanced physics at Central High School for Boys in Philadelphia. She told my mother that Paul was a genius at writing poetry, a show-off, and should go to Harvard.

"That's bullshit," I shouted to Paul about his genes. In fact, I was terrifically impressed. Years later, I would tell him that with his kinky black curls, pouty, prognathous mouth, and slanty blue eyes, he'd looked like an actor in a Hawaiian beach movie. I severely disadvantaged myself during our initial encounter—which became a shouting fight about free will and determinism—by taking off my horn-rimmed glasses to appear less the goggle-eyed bookworm.

Paul stood out among these middle-class Philadelphia Jewish kids whose parents—high-school teachers—taught us to be religious about books and the life of the mind. He was the sexiest looking in his group. Most of the boys dressed in baggy pants, cheap drip-dry shirts, and saddle shoes. He wore tight pants and tight, bright jerseys. He smoked Camel un-filtered cigarettes without inhaling, an imperfect effect that I admired. In our set he was a rare success with women. He'd had a real love affair, it was rumored, with a buxom beatnik named Norma, a Trotskyite who played the guitar and who'd actually gone to a Communist Youth Festival in Vienna. Once I turned on my television to see him doing the jitterbug on "American Bandstand." No Jewish kid from my neighborhood in North Philadelphia had ever dreamed of taking the long subway ride to the show, the turf of the tough Italian kids from South Philadelphia who *didn't* get good marks, *didn't* empty out library shelves on weekends and vacations, and who *wouldn't* (my mother pursed her lips) go to college. It was one month later after I'd visited him a few times at his after-school job at our local branch of the public library that I an-nounced to my mother that some day I was going to marry him. We were like two generals plotting a major religious war, emotionality was beneath our discussion.

"Well, he's got a lot of school ahead of him," she said and shifted our Chevrolet into reverse to back out of our driveway to go to the supermarket.

Susan at eighteen

I read a lot of books. I could make myself feel faint when I tried to think about my own or my parents' death. I didn't want to think too much about God. I felt guilty. I wasn't sure He existed. I talked about Camus's philosophy in *The Stranger.* I was proud that I had studied advanced French at Colby College one summer and worked as a busboy to pay my way. At language lab, a Parisian woman had corrected the nasal Philadelphia vowels in my French diction, a sophisticated effect for somebody who'd never been to Florida or Texas, much less France. I was tall and skinny myself, 5'9" by the time I was in the eighth grade, and I smoked cigarettes after school with my girl friends at the Esquire drugstore. We talked about our future careers. I wanted to be a lawyer, an international lawyer. We talked about getting into good colleges. I was a self-conscious intellectual snob.

Sometimes I'd take off my thick glasses and put my nose against a mirror, and I'd see the roundness of my mouth and my eyes and symmetry of my features and I'd wonder why my chopped-off hair, baggy clothes, glasses, and slouch managed to obscure this not-unpleasant-looking face. Yet I dressed the way I did because I believed that matching outfits and bright colors marked superficial women.

I was considered a leader at Girls' High School, partly because I spoke up unabashedly in meetings, often shouting out jokes without raising my hand. However, when boys visited from other high schools, I was mute. I wrote and directed the senior class show and loved ordering everybody around. At home, I resented my parents for any number of things including their refusal to send me to a college like Bryn Mawr. "Too fancy, too expensive, you're not a good enough student to deserve it. We're only a Chevrolet family," my father explained, "and that's a Cadillac college." One day I locked myself in the bathroom for eight hours, creating a problem until they agreed to let me apply to Bryn Mawr and Vassar. I wanted to go to a good school because I wanted to be "somebody important." When I won Vassar and Bryn Mawr scholarships, my genteel high school principal worried about me and other graduating seniors going to colleges like Vassar with young women from exclusive girls schools on the East Coast. Instead of taking pride in my large scholarship, I was ashamed that she'd thought that I was unfit company for these women. I thought I was lower middle-class. But I wasn't. I suppose I thought I was ugly, and I suppose I was.

The summer I turned nineteen, I made up my mind to start sleeping with Paul. I declared my decision in a long monologue to Judith, my new friend at Bryn Mawr. While I whispered to her on our kitchen phone, I worried that my mother reading her history textbooks in the living room would hear. I was designing the tactics of the romance myth I was going to construct. My relationship with Noel had ended two years before. So I told Judith that day over the phone that I had been unexpectedly depressed by the end of that relationship. As though I were pledging my life, I told her, "See, if I sleep with Paul now, it becomes a kind of marriage plan, too. Of course," and here I was choosing tactics, "I could postpone going out with him for a year to get our romance closer to our marriageable ages. But he seems so experienced that I think he sleeps with girls he goes out with."

The last was pure speculation. Back in the year 1960, I didn't know any women who admitted to having adult sex except one strange girl in my dorm who never turned in her papers and finally left school for good. We were terrified of sex, yet we wanted to be a little daring. My classmate Barbara and I giggled and worried into the early morning hours, re-smoking cigarette butts and discussing what screwing must be like. Just last year she told me she'd been lying; she'd had two abortions by our sophomore year.

Meanwhile, Paul was on a scholarship at Swarthmore College, some twenty miles from Bryn Mawr. That summer when we both returned to our Philadelphia friends, Pete Seeger concerts, and arguments about the fascism of Hollywood blacklists, I launched my campaign. I remember watching Paul jitterbug a foot or so away at a friend's wedding. "Gee, I think the sexiest things about males are their eyes and their rear ends," I announced to another boy. And then I said louder, "Paul has the nicest ass in the room." Still dancing, Paul twisted his head around, grinned at me, and flipped up the back of his baggy suit jacket. Bowled over by my own daring, I wondered if other girls had told him they liked to look at his ass. Before he left the party, he asked casually, "You got a way to get home?" Nervously, I answered, "Yeah, but thanks." Then I smiled boldly. "Thanks for thinking of me, Paul. I think of you, too."

I asked him to dance at the next party, then he followed me out onto the empty porch. While our friends inside the house sang "This Land Is Your Land," we kissed awkwardly. He seemed careful; I assumed that he didn't put a lot of energy into our necking because he didn't believe I would sleep with him.

One night we went to his father's broken-down Chevrolet and instead of starting the ignition, we kissed, straining toward each other without embarrassment. On a rainy day at his parents' tiny row house, he solemnly said he loved me. I accepted this as the sort of marvelous good fortune life should bring to everyone.

On that rainy day at his parents' house, we were lying side by side on the couch—and suddenly in his nervous grandstandy way, he picked me up and started carrying me toward a long narrow stairwell leading up to the dark bedrooms. The absurdity of Paul trying to carry someone nearly as big as himself did not detract from the seriousness of the situation. It was to be the seduction scene of my life, my touchstone, the scene that was to be evoked for me by hundreds of romantic movies, wedding announcements, glimpses of couples necking at the beach, or later by the announcements of marriages breaking up and people dating again. It was to be part of the mythology of my life. I knew I was to feel the way my mother, my teachers, and my father wanted me to feel—very little lust, but very deep love and commitment.

"What are we doing?" I asked in a whisper as he struggled to get me up the stairs. "Whatever we want to do," he answered as he heaved me along and finally into his bedroom.

As we undressed, I became more sober and scared. Looking down at my body unfamiliar on the faded old gold bedspread, I felt very lonely. Without my glasses, I could hardly see him sitting on the side of the bed. His awkward, hunched-over posture made me realize this was also hard for him, and my eyes smarted with tears of protectiveness and compassion. I sat up and rubbed his bare shoulder.

"What's the matter?"

"I'm embarrassed," he said without looking at me. "I'm just embarrassed."

When we made love I was moved, but it was physically comparable to something that would happen to me now on the gynecologist's table.

Nothing had prepared me for sex. It was partly, I suppose, my sense that this was a frightening and sinful experience that prevented my taking any physical pleasure in it. How could I enjoy anything when I was terrorized? What would my parents say if they knew?

He used condoms, taking responsibility for the act, as he would for us from then on. Afterward, he silently slipped the paper cigar band on my finger and our promise was made.

My feeling was pure love. He was tender to me, helping me put on my bra, my dungarees. He said little, putting his arm around my neck and giving me a hug. I had never loved anyone so much. In the next weeks, his presence in my life made waking up every morning a puzzle and a delight. Why am I so happy? I would think, smiling with pleasure as I rolled over in bed. And then it would come back to me. I will see Paul today. He's my boyfriend. We can make love like adults when we're alone. We can appear together at parties. I'll bask in his wit and in his perceptions. I was absorbed in the act of adoring another human being. And I think the idea that we were having sex was more important to me than the sex itself.

Soon afterward my parents decided to drive across country to visit my grandparents, who had retired to a dull sandy town below San Diego. I fought hard not to go. But back then my middle-American parents would not leave their teen-age daughter alone in a hot, lazy Philadelphia summer in an empty row house, especially a daughter who had just fallen madly in love.

Then I learned that Paul was going to California, too, a much more interesting expedition with friends who'd borrowed a car for a month. I remember our hasty good-bye and protestations of love in the teller's line at Keystone Savings Bank, where I was depositing the last salary check made at my summer job in a jewelry store. It was a stuffy day, and the dust from the streets seemed suspended in the waves of hot air. "I'll hitch down to see you from San Francisco," he promised, "or drive down with my sister. Love conquers all."

I sat sourly through most of the trip West, refusing to get out of the car to see the Grand Canyon. When we got to California there was a letter for me from Paul with a poem he had written about Southern California. Even then, there was a greedy pattern to my reading of his letters. They always appeared to be written for a more literary and literate person than myself. I would skim his love letters anxiously for any references to us or to our relationship, and failing to find the hoped-for messages, would read about how the smoggy sprawl of Los Angeles reminded him of Milton's or somebody's hell.

After many calls back and forth, it was decided that he would join me, my parents, and my grandparents for a drive to Tijuana. When he arrived with his sister, we both looked down at my feet self-consciously while he admired my rubber thong sandals, not yet sold on the East Coast. He showed me fragments of another poem he was writing, and I could tell from our smiling and looking away that things were good.

My parents were not pleased by the arrival of Paul and his sister. During the trip to Tijuana, past grape fields and sandy wastes, for some reason I had to ride once again with my family. When we parked in the hilly slum that was the center of town, we heard his sister complaining about the way he'd used the brakes of the car. It was a shock, the first realization that my gallant knight was naggable. In later domestic years, I would remember the surprise I felt then and try to evoke my romantic distance from him. We walked the tourist-filled streets of the city together. We joked about getting our pictures taken on a donkey-drawn buggy filled with fresh flowers, but I was too embarrassed to climb up there with my whole family watching. Later in the day, I bought a bookend, a small carved figure of a monk. Then we got back to our separate cars; he to return to San Francisco, my family and I to San Diego. We both knew this meeting in front of my grandparents and parents had sealed our pact a little tighter.

Back home that September, before I went off to college again, I prowled around my parents' garage for something that would make my room at college fun for him to visit. My major mood during this time was a happy trance: I was never quite listening to a conversation unless I was talking to him or about him. In the garage I found an old radio set in a cabinet, and insisted on buying it from my father, my head filled with pictures of Paul lying on my bed reading history books and listening to music.

At school, where the grass was greener and lusher than it ever got in the flat residential summer streets of Philadelphia, Paul visited me the first week. I took down from my bulletin board a yellowing and torn picture of him that I'd clipped two years before from a local Jewish newspaper: his mother had announced his prizes and scholarships on graduating from Central High School. I didn't need the picture to stare at anymore.

And so began the months of our idyll. Except for one rainy night when I came back from visiting a boyfriend from the previous semester at Haverford and found Paul glowering and soaking in the wet fall night, my dreams were expanded by the reality we made. That night I was deeply angry at him for his assumption that he had the right to reproach me. I did not want to stop seeing boys I knew, but going out and feeling "popular" meant more to me than the dullish classes I was frequently cutting or the studying I was doing to keep my scholarship average. I didn't want sex with these boys. Sex was reserved for Paul. I think I wanted to find out what it was like to grow up in Akron, Ohio, to be a Quaker, or a southern Black at Haverford. I also wanted them to like me, to find me attractive. I was beginning to make slow steps toward a real bond with Paul, I suppose, like the tin woodsman raising his hand and feeling his chest and for the first time hearing a thump. After my anger at his possessiveness passed, as we stood in the rain, I felt compassion for him and also guilt that I could be so calloused as to seek out another young man's admiring attention. Paul's should have been enough.

Every Friday night he'd come walking up my dark wide hallway about the time that the other girls were drifting out of their rooms for dinner. I'd hear his uneven footsteps in his heavy boots and a few soft female voices saying "Hiya Paul," and then he'd be in my room. We'd usually lock the door (an illegality that made me nervous) and make love or else go down to dinner and then wander the campus. Men were not allowed into rooms after 6:30, so we were at a loss for a place to go. One night we made love on the floor of a musician's practice room in the stuffy stone Gothic Goodhart Hall. Afterwards, as a joke, I went with him into the men's room, a symbolic bridge over our sexual difference. But a janitor came running in after me to say, "You're not allowed in here. Get out." I was mortified.

Those afternoons in my room, we'd fall asleep hugging each other on the narrow cot and wake up to hear the dinner buzzer and the sounds of girls laughing and wandering down the winding paths on the green rolling campus. The college looked, when I remembered to register it for memories, like a picture postcard, too good to be real. A year later in the summer I wandered back to campus with Paul to look at the empty stone buildings, and the tiny dark dormitory room that was my whole life in winter. He discovered that a window to my room was open and volunteered to help me climb in. I wouldn't let him, suddenly conscious that I was part of a community out here with some rules that I musn't let him disobey. Those fall and winter afternoons in that tiny space in that suburban Philadelphia copy of Oxford and Cambridge were among the happiest of my life. I was too dazed to compare this feeling and relationship I had with Paul to anything in the past, and I was too innocent to worry about the future. I would usually cry after we made love; we were coming apart and being two separate people again. Because I never confided to anyone about my sex life with him I half-believed he and I had invented this way of bringing two people close.

During the first winter we were dating, reality intruded. Paul used to borrow a friend's car to come to visit me at Bryn Mawr when his motorscooter and his ski mask weren't guard enough against the snow and wind. One night he appeared in a strange jalopy; the car's seats were torn, and the muffler had a hole in it. After a movie we drove up Montgomery Pike to Bryn Mawr; the sort of suburban road where the supermarkets are brick colonial. I was teeth-chatteringly cold.

As he and I both started fumbling for the heater control, we slammed into the back of a parked car at sixty miles an hour. After a few seconds when I could see him moving, I felt only relief. That meant that he and I had both survived. I don't remember ever hearing the crash. My shoulder ached. My tooth had a new jagged edge. I looked closely at Paul. He was irrevocably changed—his two front teeth were badly broken. It made me nauseated.

It was after this he passed my final test. All through the next week I felt as though something had ended, as if some great mood or feeling had passed. When he appeared the next Friday, I looked at him desperately. With his two front teeth chipped, he looked like a parody of himself. And I knew I'd made a terrible mistake trusting myself to him. We'd gotten into a traffic accident, and that seemed an overpowering sign that we did not belong together. Maybe he could not take care of me, nor I of him. I wanted to get away from him. I don't remember what I said, but I think I told him that I wasn't sure if I loved him. He got a sad, high-pitched sound in his voice, but he nodded and said, "I know, I know, sometimes you just forget you love a person," and then he sat down on my bed and pulled off his boots. "Sometimes making love is the best way to remember," he said quietly. Later, I walked him to the train in silence. I had cried more this time during our lovemaking. My tears were partly the return of my tenderness toward him and partly fear. I knew that if he didn't leave me because of this awful confession of mine, he was bound to me forever. I also knew that making the confession was a great effort for me, my way of asking for his help, and he'd given it.

Wedding

The wedding was the inevitable and frightening event that I had been moving toward and away from since I first slept with Paul at age nineteen. When he slipped the cigar band on my finger, I figured it would come in the future. But for me the future never arrived smoothly. Emerson said that people should be very careful in deciding what they want in life because they almost certainly will achieve it.

During our junior year of college, somebody—Paul or I—brought up marriage. It was after visiting a couple at Swarthmore who were living off campus in a tiny apartment with candles, a few pieces of silver, wedding gifts, paintings, a couch covered in an Indian-print bedspread and basically no money in the place, but lots of taste. There was also a crib with an occupant in a tiny room off the living room.

I remember a subsequent visit to my dean in which she wearily stated that I could transfer credits to Swarthmore where Paul was a student, if I wanted, or else I could continue as a Bryn Mawr student. Her mild disapproval was obvious. She was fortyish and tended toward fitted green suits with A-line skirts, saddle shoes, bushy eyebrows, horn-rimmed glasses, and archaeological digs around the world every summer. I never even understood the impact of the disapproval of this woman who had chosen a single life enriched by a study of the past. Instead, as I walked over the grassy lawns back to my dormitory, I decided that my perpetual panic at the thought of marriage had made the interview go strangely. I know now that women like my dean must have made some impression on me and my college friends. She lived alone, traveled alone. I remember the awe I felt when we visited her apartment on campus, decorated with bookshelves and archaeological stones. But my female friends and I had already been formed by our mothers and our early education, so much so that we joked contemptuously about the favorite saying of Bryn Mawr's founder, M. Carey Thomas, "Only our failures marry."

It was this year, my junior year, that Paul and I decided to tell my parents that we were to be married. He and I drove from our suburban campuses back into the city into my neighborhood and to the dark street that I pretended was a movie set of my past because seeing it as a place where children and parents still lived was too painful. I remember announcing to my parents with nervous dread only the nuts and bolts of our decision. We would get an apartment at Swarthmore and I would transfer credits. My father got up a few times to get a drink of water, which I suspect was laced with Scotch, and then sat in silence. My mother marked a few papers for her class, did her knitting and nodded. It was as unjoyous and unceremonial as a situation could be. And I also felt a growing fear that we were talking about something that would never happen. I felt numb toward Paul.

In the car once again, we decided to go to see the film, *L'Avventura,* at a nearby suburban shopping center. On the way to the movie I stole a look at a silent Paul driving the car in his unfamiliar and poorly fitted suit. As I watched him, I fixed on his hairline. Someday he would be bald. I wanted to escape. Did I need the responsibility of growing old with a man? A man whose hair would eventually be gone. I saw only visions of decay and loss. At the movie I silently despaired as I watched the story unfold about the boring lives of vapid people who couldn't locate or love each other. Once more I was certain this marriage would never take place. We stopped seeing each other that spring; the tension of planning our future made us snap at each other with new angers as each tallied the other's imperfections.

That summer every time someone in our Philadelphia group of friends mentioned him, I'd feel a sense of loss. Where was he? We'd meet tentatively at parties and then usually I'd make the first move, aware of his smiles and pregnant looks and soon we were telephoning and seeing each other again.

We seemed to do this for the next two years. When we were "broken up" I'd try to start dating new men. At first it seemed like a great idea. Getting to know a new person, and getting flattering attention. But a few weeks after the initial glow, I'd start feeling lonely. The new guy wasn't Paul, he lacked his tenderness or wit, and I'd break off the relationship. Often our breakup would occur because Paul would become so involved with his exams that he wouldn't have time to see me. I'd interpret this as rejection and so we'd fight and break up—with me refusing to admit to him and even to myself that I'd rejected him out of childish fear.

So I spent three years making plans with Paul, going into

a panic over the enormity of the decision to marry, breaking up with him, and then quietly finding my way back into a relationship with a reliable and loving friend. My worries would include hours of wondering whether I actually wanted to spend the rest of my life looking across the breakfast table at him. The idea of committing a whole lifetime to an emotional tie made me feel numb. He would answer my nervous questions, "Just think about life in five-year chunks even when you say forever."

The final decision was made on a wintry Philadelphia street near the apartment in which I was living, while studying philosophy at Penn graduate school. After yet another reconciliation, we were now reduced to long late-night telephone conversations and occasional weekend visits between Philadelphia and New Haven where he was studying English political history. I brought up the subject, testing him to see if *he* wanted to get married, still unsure of myself. We were talking about friends of his who were married graduate students in New Haven. "I bet it'd be more fun living that way than alone," I mused out loud. "Why don't you think about it?" "Would you like to get married?" he asked quickly. "I mean you're the only person I could think of marrying at this point." There it was. My proposal. And among all the reactions I felt, I nurtured for years a small hurt that he didn't ask me with high romance.

I suggested that I come to live in New Haven without benefit of a marriage ceremony, but quickly agreed with him that this wouldn't be quite right. Since I was of about six minds about the entire affair, I would have felt hurt if he'd agreed with my suggestion. I wondered what I was committing myself to, listening to my voice telling relatives over the telephone, "Paul and I have decided to get married." I felt my fears were routine since I had made the plans so many times. What was unrecognizable was my voice making the announcements and Paul's plan to work for the city of Philadelphia that summer to get an extra thousand dollars for us to live on.

My mother was relieved that I finally was going to take the big step. She felt it was her role to take such plans seriously no matter how fickle I'd been in the past.

For the ceremony she found a semi-retired rabbi who lived in a huge, rambling old house in which he performed marriages. Two of my closest girl friends had also decided to get married that summer. I joked that it was the thing to do, but I was relieved that I had two people with whom I could compare fears and irritations.

My mother was bothered partly because she felt she had so little time to prepare, despite the three-year warning. My friend Alice's mother had banished her to Atlantic City where she had to lie in the sun for eight hours a day in order to achieve a tan that would set off her white satin dress. Also, Alice's mother was spending several thousand dollars for a photographer, whereas my mother seemed quite happy to let eager relatives or friends take pictures, thus reducing the formality of the occasion. The final problem that Alice had was that in a rehearsal the rabbi and her mother decided that her push-up bra exposed an amount of cleavage inappropriate to an altar; she was allowed two minutes between the ceremony and the receiving line to change from a regular bra to a push-up bra. Luckily I was so surly and unpredictable that nobody dared make me face these problems.

On the day of the wedding the rabbi interviewed me for five minutes before the ceremony. He found out I had studied philosophy and I told him I thought the ceremony was unimportant; that the major event had been making the decision to marry. About a half hour before the ceremony his wife took my hand and pulled me into the large living room with a stage at one end. She showed me a curtain decorated with an oil painting of Moses on the Mount which at a musical signal would separate and lift, revealing the bride. When I told her that I didn't want to stand behind the curtain, she was somewhat pitying, explaining that "All the girls love to do it, and the newspapers always give it a big write-up."

I remember little of the ceremony. I was told to walk slowly down the aisle with my father, stepping majestically to every other beat of Mendelssohn's wedding march. But when my time came, I rushed down the aisle, dragging my father behind me. I watched faces from my childhood—aunts, mothers, friends—watching me. The rabbi said I was deep because I studied philosophy and because I knew that the decision to marry was more important than the ceremony. Paul pronounced his "I do" with great fervor, the same energy he displayed when he danced his sexy twist. I noted that Paul was extroverted enough to enjoy this public bonding.

After the ceremony we repaired to another room lined with patterned green velvet wallcovering where my elderly aunts with their darkening teeth and satin suits talked behind their hands to each other and watched my friends self-consciously group and regroup. I found myself whirling around the room, accepting congratulations and hugs.

The main thing was that it didn't hurt at all. I now wore on my left hand this heavy gold band that my father had unearthed from some secret place in his bureau drawer. It reminded me of a photograph of my mother holding me as a baby in which a strong left hand is bracing a pudgy baby's chest. On that hand is her ring, a simple, strong symbol of her role as the wife and mother. Looking across at Paul, I still felt numb, but my feelings would return. We had accomplished this amazingly complicated series of acts together, and having him as my husband seemed a good idea—as it would seem for years afterward.

Now, looking back, I see that when I got married I was lost. I had spent the year before at graduate school, reading Mary McCarthy novels and worrying about my waning interest in philosophy, a subject I had enjoyed at Bryn Mawr. I was also scared about how I would make a living. Reading Kant as an undergraduate had been exotic. Here was a man who pondered whether external reality was more than the minds that perceived it, a whimsical question that titillated me and my sense that things were less clear than most people believe. But in graduate school I felt pedantic making syllogisms and counter examples out of his books, memorizing arguments and rereading texts and critiques. When I sat down to study, I found myself daydreaming instead about buying a velvet bathrobe or visiting Paul up in New Haven, or making a telephone call to Alice who was then a graduate student at Berkeley.

In my senior year of college I had doodled on my notebooks, "Please God let me be accepted at graduate school. *Je veux un avenir.*" Without something to do, I was nothing. When I was fifteen, my mother had raised her eyebrows at me and pronounced, "All the boys you know seem to have future vocations. You seem lost." When I discovered philosophy, I felt saved. But then in graduate school, I was again lost. I studied so little that I felt as though I was lying when people asked me what I did and I answered, "I'm a graduate student in philosophy at Penn." Marrying was a way out, a way to find an identity for myself. If I couldn't be a graduate student of philosophy, I could be a wife. Of course, when I left Penn I arranged to transfer my credits and take courses at Yale, but at bottom I felt dread: I was lying to myself about my interest in reading philosophy.

Instead of going on a honeymoon, Paul decided that we would save money by simply living at his parents' house for two weeks before we set out for New Haven. I was disappointed in the lack of private celebration this implied but proud of him for being unconventional. But I did feel sorry for myself when the night we got married Paul's cousin walked in on me while I was in the bathroom in his parents' house.

I felt foolish, a little ugly, and suddenly deprived. It just seemed that I hadn't the necessary private good moments either with Paul or even by myself that should follow on the public event of our wedding. When his mother grabbed the dishes out of my hand after dinner one night, saying with embarrassment, "You shouldn't be doing these now," again I felt a little sad, thinking, "Yes, by all conventions I should be having a glorious vacation somewhere in some romantic setting." I blamed him for not arranging such a context, but I didn't mention it. I didn't want to hurt his feelings. I also didn't want to upset the idea that we were now happy.

It was one week after our wedding that Alice got married in a ceremony including color-coordinated flower girls, her suntan, and her push-up bra in the receiving line. After an opulent dinner at her parents' synagogue, she changed into a suit and hat and we all waved good-bye. A few hours later she called me up at Paul's parents' house to ask gaily, "What's up? We're at the Holiday Inn and we're bored." I wondered then if all honeymoons were disappointing, and maybe it was just as well Paul and I hadn't spent any money.

SEPTEMBER

September 1: Evening

Yesterday my telephone rang, and as soon as I heard Jim's voice, I kept thinking: No, I must not even talk to him. After the first few seconds, I began to hear his words. "Is that you? Hon, you been fine, I expect? I'm playin' in New York City, and I'm inviting you to the Americana Motel where I am currently in residence."

"Well, I'm actually busy today." My negative answer made me feel virtuous.

"Now hon, now don't be doing me like that. I'm only human, remember feelin' my heart, don't you?" As his words trailed off uncertainly, he sounded less like a hustler. I wondered why I was treating him as the enemy. After all, nothing bad had happened to me as a result of our last encounter, so why not see him again? My article on him has not appeared yet. If I saw him I could update it and give it a New York City peg. I wouldn't have to sleep with him.

"Well, I'm not sure," I hedged. "How long are you going to be in New York?" I hadn't planned my words, and I was surprised as I heard them tumbling out.

"Ooh hon, please," and his formal manners were dropped and his voice trembled with hurt pride, "I am askin' you to come to see me. Now I have debated a lot about whether this was a good idea. I nearly did not call you. But I decided yes. You there?"

"Yes," I heard my voice sounding more pliant.

"Then come on by right now. It'll be good, you see."

"Where are you?" I meant to answer indifferently, but I could hear my voice sounding softer.

"Americana Motel."

"If I can, I'll come over," I said, pretending I was postponing the decision. Pretending, but fooling neither of us.

In the two minutes after Jim hung up, I had combed my hair, put on a clean red blouse, and decided not to wash my face. I muttered a lie to Paul while I wrestled my coat on. It's getting easier to lie to him.

"I'm meeting Judith for a Coke. See you later." I kissed his forehead, wishing I could protect him from the things I do behind his back.

In the cab, because I couldn't even imagine the scene I was entering, I weighed the abstract question: meeting strange men in Americana Motel rooms is—or is not—dirty. So what's wrong with dirty anyway? I won't be killed or crippled by it. What can it hurt? I spent all those years straining for middle-class cleanliness, feeling my braces on my teeth were never expensive or painful enough, eating my boiled carrots, sneaking only a rare ice cream soda, refusing to admit that I could have sex until I was sure I would marry the young man in question, and then pretending to everyone else I was still a virgin. I am always trying to live up to rules, rules that circumscribe fun. And since I am married, I must refuse to admit the existence of any man's penis except my husband's. I have lived a life of moral superiority, a fact I had never recognized, so impressed was I with the impossibility of my standards. One act of adultery has not sullied my clean-cut history.

Maybe I am just a silly housewife having a fling. It's

true that Jim is the only man besides my husband that I ever slept with and that's reason enough to see him again. I don't remember why I did sleep with him. I won't want to sleep with him again. I can't wait to see him, to sort all this out.

The measuring looks in the eyes of the men in the red-carpeted lobby flash at me like danger lights on a highway. These short-haired salesmen, dwarfed by the gaudy chandeliers, wear their convention buttons proudly. I believe that if I acknowlege their smiles or greetings, they will feel contempt for me, that I'm too easy, a prostitute. My footsteps make no noise on the paisley wall-to-wall carpet. I feel self-conscious, unsure I am taking a step in my own life. Maybe I'm acting in a play where self-confident gestures are all the situation demands.

Adultery requires self-deception. You have to keep convincing yourself that momentary pleasure won't cause you or your husband later pain. You tell yourself this so you won't become catatonic while greeting this black-eyed gremlin whose gray velours jumpsuit matches the melancholy hollows under his eyes. He jumps up from the unmade bed, kicking his guitar with a resounding thud, and bends down to kiss my hands, saying, "I am so pleased, so pleased. I did not believe you would come, I truly didn't."

Looking down at the top of his lush black pompadour, I feel my face twitch, but the phone rings and then only I am paying attention to me. As I pretend to stare at the guitar on the bed, Jim is yelling into the phone, "Aah don't care what they say. You're doin' publicity for me, and you tell them I'm goin' t'be a star, y'hear? And I want mah rightful place on that-there marquee. Why, did you see me and my mammy doin' the Johnny Cash show? She cried for all of America to see on that show." He turns and grins at me, pulling my arm hard so that I am sitting next to him on the messy bed. I look down at his skinny thighs covered with the velours.

I feel like a spectator in my own life. What will I do next? He hangs up the telephone and turns to me, idly stroking my arm. "Hungry, darling?" he asks, staring at the telephone. Never, I assure myself, never will I be sexually attracted to, much less actually screw this freak madman egomaniac. "Help yourself to some liquor." He gestures toward the bottle of bourbon. "Room service is bringing us two club sandwiches any minute." And then he walks into the bathroom.

I am unsettled. What if he gets really mad because I won't sleep with him? He greeted me indifferently, and he's dressed in flashy gray velvet. How obnoxious he is ordering around his publicity man, and who gives him the right to make me sit down on his bed? I want out. I want to go home and talk to people who share my history, who will know things I know, who will talk to me the way they've learned over the years that I want to be talked to. I gulp down two stinging sips of bourbon, a taste I can't stand.

He returns, humming a nasal Johnny Cash melody and I wish I could hear it better. But he's wearing only a towel around his waist and I am scared. "I feel like leaving," I say sullenly. "Aww hon," and he's standing close to me, the afternoon sun is gone and nobody has turned on the lights. He's stroking my arms gently, and I'm relaxing. It's only the liquor, I tell myself. "I truly want to be your friend. I truly don't know how to talk with you. Help me to learn. We have a lot of getting to know each other to do. Don't be runnin' off." He raises his sad dark eyes to stare into mine, a flagrantly melodramatic gesture, but I am moved.

"You're not the type of gal who just gets a man goin' in order to turn him down?" he asks, moving his thin-lipped mouth up toward mine.

Paul's mouth is soft, I tell myself.

As he touches my back, I shiver, hating him for helping me to break my promise to Paul. Jim holds my shoulders, looking at my face. He's shaking me gently. "You're very smart and you've read more books than me, hon. But I can tell you better how ah feel. I feel we'all have an emotional thing—a sadness and a joy together." My thoughts are jangled. Is this a place my life has been heading? Is this wild, sad-eyed man ever going to look like someone I know? How will I feel later when I see him on stage or in another room?

September 10: Morning

I am losing weight. It's this business of going to Jim's hotel room every day this week in the afternoons and watching him at night while he shouts into a microphone and jumps around the stage. My work is not suffering. I am an obsessive journalist, and like any new convert (I didn't care about my work until I started writing for a New Haven newspaper at the age of twenty-four) I am overzealous.

In New Haven, I began to hate my philosophy classes and to despair over what I would do with my life. I don't know why I chose newspapers. Maybe it was because creative writing was the only course I'd loved at college. While I was writing my weekly stories I'd forget that time was passing. I applied to the *New Haven Register,* the city's afternoon paper, after I'd gotten a chill reading the obituary of a female reporter. The big point the writer made was that the reporter would rarely take seriously a no-comment or a refusal to be interviewed. She'd show up or ask the difficult question anyway—and get the story. The idea that a woman could be so brave pleased me; I was tired of being brave by pretending to like the abstractions of linguistic philosophy. I wanted to see the world and to write about it.

The personnel director of the *Register* saw me as another minor problem when I showed him my three best short stories and my resume. He said, "On the one hand you're overqualified, on the other hand you're underqualified." He didn't like the looks of me. I didn't like watching him running his fingers through his bright orange-colored crew cut. I told him I would do anything—typing, filing—anything just to work on a newspaper. I thought of myself as Rosalind Russell in *His Girl Friday*. I'd decided that newspaper people admire nerve and aggressiveness. But I think my zeal for what he considered a pedestrian life embarrassed the man. He hired me reluctantly as an assistant typist.

For three months I typed names and addresses of employees on file cards. All my efforts to get free-lance, unpaid assignments from the all-male city desk editors were met with sturdy refusals. Then I discovered that the women's page editor, a sweet-faced woman with ten photographs of cats under the glass top of her desk, would let me rewrite letters announcing marriages and engagements into *Register* style and type them up. For about three weeks I did this during my lunch hour and was thrilled. The women's page editor told me that book reviews were considered so inconsequential at the *Register* that writers were not paid to do them. So I politely hounded the book review editor until he let me take a novel to review that he had been planning to throw away. Paul read the review when I was finished and added a flourish at the end. The editor liked it and offered me another book. My woman friend told me dryly that the only rule she knew in journalism was to write an interesting lead paragraph. "That's all people read around here," she assured me. I didn't believe her cynicism, but I spent what felt like hours on my leads. I wrote the reviews with the excitement I'd felt with my short stories. I'd forgotten I could be that interested in working. I pinned them up on the wall near my typewriter until there were too many of them.

Later the book editor agreed with my suggestion that I write a profile of Yale's activist chaplain Reverend William Sloan Coffin for the Sunday magazine section that was filled with wire service pictures of tame tigers and the bodies of bosomy actresses and muscle-bound actors. He paid me $25 for the Coffin story and never raised my rates over the next two years. I covered Yale people and events for him. It would take me several hours of research—reading the first novel of a southwestern writer in residence or the law review articles of Eugene Rostow. Then I would type a list of fifty questions for my subject and for as many of his students or colleagues as I could find.

I was fired from the *Register* a scant three months after I was hired, disgraced because I didn't type the cards fast enough. I took another job doing "internal public relations" —designing elevator cards and putting out a magazine for retired employees of the local telephone company. I continued to write features for the *Register* magazine during lunch hours, Sundays, and at night when Paul was first writing his thesis and then his articles on Cromwell's involvement with the English revolution.

My mother had always had plans for my life's work, even before I developed my newspaper obsession. When it became clear that I loved to tame the wild cats at my aunt's farm we'd visit each summer, she suggested I grow up to become a veterinarian. Unsurprising choice for a Jewish mother who herself was a high-school teacher who'd gotten to college on a scholarship. This was all despite her Jewish patriarchal father who believed that girls were not worth educating. Of course my mother knew I shouldn't aspire to be a people doctor; that would be the role of my brother or the man I would marry. But the intelligent if lazy female, reasoned mother, could doctor animals. "You'd make a good living," she advised one day.

These world-shaping pronouncements were always made modestly, while she was dealing herself a game of solitaire on the kitchen table, sipping tea from a glass the way her Russian father used to, or reluctantly scraping at a cucumber for our dinner. She never looked at me during these moments of instruction and confrontation, but her sighing would continue, "So you'd have a skill, be able to set your own hours, and you'd be a professional person after only four years of college. And you could work any place, any place your, aah, husband's work took him."

Of course my work would be secondary. My husband's would be the brilliant career. It would be up to him to forge it, up to me to find him, and though I didn't see it then—up to me not to be jealous of his success.

To her credit, along with hundreds of guilts and inadequate feelings, my mother inspired in me a necessary feeling that I had to discover a métier, a way of earning my keep. She despaired of my ever finding it because in the 1950s and 1960s we both believed that the answer should come through my school work. I didn't love any course at college except creative writing, which I never thought could lead to a career.

September 16

Yesterday I sprawled on Jim's bed while he walked around and around the bed and talked his life story into a microphone. It seems some educational television producer wants to make a movie about him. I heard anecdotes about feeding chickens on the houseboat on the Mississippi with his "mammy," about how he wasn't weaned until he was five, about how he didn't speak English until he was seven. "Why not stay for dinner?" he asked at five o'clock. I pulled the telephone onto my chest and called Paul. I am maintaining the fiction that I am researching my article. "Okay, honey." Paul sounded as though he was thinking about something else. "I'll grab a bite here and see you later. Say, is that him talking in the background?" "Yes." In fact Jim was gesturing dramatically with one hand and cuddling the microphone with the other while he confided his tales in his most dramatic Johnny Cash rumble. Paul was impressed. "He has the sexiest speaking voice I've ever heard. Does he have a cold?"

September 17

Besides arranging our weddings for the same week five years ago, Alice and I have arranged our lives so that her apartment where she lives with her husband and two children is directly beneath Paul's and mine. Last night before I left home at eleven to hear Jim's last show, Alice tugged on a clump of my hair. "You are so high and happy lately. What's your secret?" she asked. I have not told her about Jim. Telling Judith was disloyal enough to Paul. But since she lives downstairs, Alice sees us both too often to know this.

September 19

Today, Jim handed me a small packet in cellophane with a blank look on his face and shrugged as I squeezed the white powder inside it. "What is this?" I asked. "Oh, somebody handed it to me last night after dinner." He shrugged again. "It's cocaine, honey. Ya inta it?" "No." I was self-assured. "You shouldn't be hanging around this hotel with this stuff. I mean a musician and all would be the first person they'd bust." "Whatever you think," he said, his back to me, and humming a little under his breath he was watching himself in the mirror and wiping an imaginary spot off his chin.

"I'll flush it down the toilet," I announced, as though I was a member of a Salvation Army marching band. "Okay," he said.

I wonder if Jim thinks I'm crazy. He does accept me now, as a voyeur. At night, I can be chatting at a sedate cocktail party with friends or sitting at home in front of my typewriter, but when the clock starts moving toward eleven, I often casually begin the same rationalization. Why not hail a cab and rush down to that basement hovel called The Nightspot and sit there in the dark with my untouched Coca-Cola and stamp my foot as I watch him stomp and scream and moan through his one-hour show. Paul doesn't seem to mind, and I suppose it's some temporary weirdness on my part. Jim is leaving in a few weeks anyway.

Afternoons, it's the getting to know him, not even the act of sex itself. Sometimes I feel almost nothing as he first kisses me; fearful that I will be too anxiety-ridden to be able to go through with it. It's after a few hugs and smiles that I finally relax. Oddly, the sex is so intense and new, but I never feel I love him like I love Paul. At other times I hate Jim for assuming that I will arrive day after day, that he can ignore me, invite other women along with us, order me around ("You're gonna pick up that telephone and tell them honey, that you are callin' for me," thumb to his chest, "and ah want mah green suit cleaned pronto.") Sometimes I hate the shortness of his legs, the fake quiver of emotion in his voice when he thinks he should appear more moved than he feels, the cunning look he gets in his eye, and the sneer that appears on his mouth when he talks about money and how he wants more.

But I do love the emotional explosions of our afternoons. He cried yesterday and so did I as we each wondered out loud if we'd meet again after this trip. Maybe I am touched by Jim because I've been involved so long with Paul who takes care of me, who rationally explains away my up and down moods, who never needs *me* to pat *his* shoulder because he's crying about me or about anything.

Paul acts sometimes as though he's the keeper and I'm the mental case. I'm less emotional than Jim, so I can take care of him a little. Yesterday, I watched him packing up his laundry and grinned. "Soon you'll be doing that without this audience." I meant that he was leaving New York and me. "Yeah? You gonna miss me," he answered, bending over the hotel laundry bag. "Maybe I will," I teased him. He threw the last jacket on the floor, and started to shout. "Aw, then why not get the hell outa here and get it over with?" Then he wasn't shouting anymore, but sitting sadly on the side of the bed. I felt awful that I'd been so flip, but I was pleased finally to see him smile a little as I wrapped my arms around his neck and rocked him a little from side to side.

This afternoon he sat up angrily after we made love and shrugged off my comforting pat with a histrionic gesture of his shoulder. He lit one of his menthol cigarettes and started to complain. It seems that his brother has called him and told him that Jim's wife is going out dancing a lot. "Well, I doubt if it's true," I comforted him, surprised by my desire to see him happier. No jealousy about his wife. "Anyway, while you're up here with me, maybe she should go dancing," I continued. "Aw, you're ignorant about some things, honey, despite all them books you looked through. No matter what, a man still feels real bad, if his wife is running around on him."

"She's running around on herself," I answered.

September 21

I keep coming back night after night. I huddle in my coat, clap my hands, and stare and marvel that I've actually done it. I have on my own contracted to commit adultery.

I want to understand. I must sit here in the dark and stare at him and wonder why *him,* what is his place in my life.

Sometimes after applause (we in the audience for the last show never number more than twenty-five) that resounds like isolated street noise on a hot New York night, he will stride out through the emptying room, hugging and blowing kisses madly. Ignoring me, he'll pull several embarrassed and exalted women along with him. After a few minutes of feeling deserted, I will wander into the all-night bar a few doors down the tawdry Village street. Sure enough, he's usually seated at the huge round table, talking about religion. ("Mah pappy showed me all the religion I ever needed. 'Son,' he said, 'as long as you take care of yourself, the Lord takes care of his own.'") Or maybe he's discoursing on patriotism with an ironic motion of his eyebrow. (" 'The Star-Spangled Banner' is a great tune. I'd dance to it any day of the week.") For a few minutes I stand ignored and shamed at his elbow. Then finally, one of the women at the table darts a nervous look at my face, takes pity on me, and says, "Hello." "Hello," I answer mournfully.

"Oh hiya, hon," Jim will say without turning around. "Pull up a chair for her," he tells his manager, "and get yourself a drink now." And I sit and drink my Coke and wonder if he's got a crush on any of these ladies—tonight they're dark-eyed Italian women, hairdressers from a beauty parlor in New Jersey. It seems one of them once wrote to Jim so he wrote back, and soon he was sending photographs of himself, and they were hanging them up in the beauty parlor. One woman went so far as to paint his portrait in water colors on a canvas shaped like a guitar. As I sit watching him, he rewards me for my vigil, and gives me a quick nod after he's drawn out an excruciating series of good-nights, and God bless, God bless. We take a cab to the Americana, where he gets out. I tell him good-night and take the cab home.

September 23

A week ago Judith took me aside and told me, "You better stop playing those Jim St. Clare records. Night and day, they're going full force in this house. If I were Paul, I'd really be pissed off." She was wrong. Since she knew about Jim and me, she was using information about me that Paul did not know. I don't agree with her, but I'm going to think about it. The idea of Paul angry or threatened is preposterous to me. I assume he figures I'm working when I see Jim. Sometimes I wish he would be passionately angry, jealous. He's so adult and controlled, I feel like a maniac by comparison. Would I want my wife running off nights to hear some fiddler yodel and wail in a seedy Village bar and then hopping around the house during the day to his records going full blast? No, maybe she's right. I'm being selfish.

September 30

Last night was Jim's final show. Paul and I and two other couples arranged to eat a Chinese dinner in the Village and then walk over to hear him play and sing. My asking Paul to come doesn't make me as nervous as it might have a few weeks ago. Last Wednesday Jim told me abruptly that he'd decided I would go on the road with him and become his manager. I managed to tell him that I was a writer and a wife with a life in New York. I couldn't help but think he made the suggestion just as I was becoming used to the idea that he was leaving in a week. I am no longer jealous of

women hanging around him after showtime, and have begun
to go down there less. "Aw, you got me going," Jim said
sadly, "so you don't even have to worry about me at all." I
do feel like I've been through a bout of a disease that gave me
a strong fever for three or four weeks. Now that I'm recover-
ing, I don't really want to recall the intensity.

I don't feel as guilty toward Paul either. I know I can't
confess to him what I've done, but I believe that the gap
will close behind this incident and leave our marriage okay.

At the show, we were the bulk of the audience. In the
dark I saw Paul once press his fingers to his ears, as an ampli-
fier went out and started to ring. I was hoping Jim would do
well. But I think he was trying too hard; he'd turned up the
electric bass and guitar so loud that sometimes I couldn't
hear his voice.

After the show was over, Paul leaned over the table
covered with glasses and peanuts and said, "Let's go and meet
Jim. He's good." I had only been backstage once myself, the
night the photographer had come to take Jim's picture for my
piece. I felt that it was intruding. But I agreed. I was embarrassed as we walked to the front of the tiny room, conscious
that I hadn't invited the other couples. But then I turned and
saw they were behind us. A waiter winked at me and I ducked
my head. Did he suspect that Jim and I were involved? Would
Paul sense this?

Backstage, Jim was talking earnestly to a waitress clutching her tray to her chest. Then I wondered how Jim would
treat Paul. By his standards, this meeting should probably not
even take place. I remembered the angry tone in his voice
when he talked about his wife going out dancing.

Jim was wearing a velvet bathrobe opened a little too
dangerously to his stomach, and he smelled of fresh sweat
and violets. Paul shook his hand hard, and even clasped his
shoulder with his other hand. He kept saying, "I like your
show, it's all right. I like your show." Paul was wearing a

tweed jacket I'd helped him pick out at the Yale Coop, black-rimmed glasses, and a button-down striped shirt and rumpled navy tie. He looked clean, studenty, and sweet. Jim nodded and smiled and said, "Glad to see you, make your acquaintance. I was beginning to wonder if you did exist." I got a flicker of fear as he opened up the subject of my potential singleness. Would Paul be forced to comment on all my solitary vigils at concerts? But Jim continued, "You've got a good wife. Yes sir, a good wife there."

I was touched by Paul's ability to handle the situation. He's so kind—and look what I put him through. Later he made me cry when he confided on the subway home, "I shook his hand really hard, and looked him right in the eye. I knew that would be important to someone like him. Don't you think? I mean, he probably puts a lot of stock into how hard guys shake his hand."

NOVEMBER

November 3

Yesterday as I sat formally on the edge of a yellow chair talking with Gloria Steinem in her apartment, I found myself blurting out, "Sometimes my marriage feels confining." She nodded her head, but answered, "Yet you said he helps you with your work." I was shocked. I'd never said that Paul was less than perfect before. I was consulting her about taking a part-time job at *Glamour* magazine, writing a by-line feature story every month. I had decided to ask her advice because she used to write for *Glamour* and because I had found her wise and warm when I interviewed her once last year.

She urged me to write for all those female *Glamour* readers rather than take a full-time job at *Newsweek,* which I've also been tentatively offered. She repeated her maxim: It's hard to be a free-lance writer without a little part-time steady income—either editing, writing, or consulting to one magazine. She said that *Newsweek* writers don't get by-line credits. "If you write for them you'll be anonymous. You should be doing your own writing and getting credit for it. You'll have little time to do your own work with a full-time *Newsweek* job. I bet you're getting that old lonely feeling sitting home by yourself writing every day." She smiled. "Go to *Glamour* for a few days a week."

I walked home across the park, brooding over my disloyal remark about my marriage. If I cover a political movement, an event or a person, I can't really get involved because of Paul. I did spend three weeks hanging around Jim. But when dinnertime comes and everybody starts arguing about their favorite restaurant, I usually go home. I save my secrets, except for my meetings with Jim, for Paul, too. We are institutionalized confidantes. I am a dependent person. I bet Gloria Steinem isn't. I don't think one person must stand by and give her support, she can carry her own center around with her. Maybe I'm wrong. Maybe a married person could accomplish this too. All I know is I feel I could vomit when I try to imagine losing Paul's approval.

DECEMBER

December 20

At *Glamour* magazine I feel for the first time in two years as though I have a real job, though I have been making around $10,000 a year free-lancing. I enjoy the Monday morning editorial meetings and the sense that I am helping to produce a product, although at last week's faculty cocktail party in the N.Y.U. book-lined reception room I was embarrassed to tell two of Paul's colleagues about my new job. I feel it makes me sound frivolous. The other day when I interviewed a doctor who writes adventure books, he looked me up and down as I took off my coat in his stuffy suite at the Hotel Algonquin. I felt the interview was underpinned with this gleam in his eye which said, "Wow, I'm in New York and in the superficial glamour circuit where girls come and ask me questions for silly slick magazines."

Yesterday in an editorial meeting at *Glamour,* one editor announced, "We need a rock story." I felt uneasy; rock reminds me of Jim St. Clare. We were sitting in what looks like a fantasy dorm room with candy-striped wallpaper, fresh pink flowers, smiling dolls, cushions, and happy pictures. "Didn't you just do a rock story, Susan?" I stopped doodling black ink circles within circles and looked up.

"Marriages are breaking up right and left. *Women Today* magazine has asked us to recommend a couple with two successful careers," interrupted another editor, patting her starched collar. "Susan has a good two-career marriage," she said. "Let's get her and her husband to tell all."

She looked at me kindly. I did not smile back.

The editor-in-chief wandered by my desk today to remind me about the *Women Today* article. I dialed Paul's number at N.Y.U. to put the question to him. He was enthusiastic about the idea of getting our pictures and thoughts in a magazine. I haven't told him I am frightened that it would mean taking a very close look at something as important and mysterious as our marriage. (After all, I am also reminded of my euphoria when at the age of ten I got my picture in our local paper, riding a circus elephant.) I won't think about Jim St. Clare. Why should I? That episode was a fluke. It proved that Paul and I are stronger than any passing fancy. But I wonder if we can afford to present our "two-career marriage" for public inspection. I am not sure I want anyone else to look closely at the good and bad parts of my life. Of course, being in the business of giving other people publicity doesn't reduce the allure of it. Yet as my father said gloomily on the phone tonight, giving me a start of fear, "Nothing good can come of bragging in public about a marriage."

JANUARY

January 3

The interviewer came to our apartment with tape recorder and questions. I realized I would lie by omission about my affair. Maybe I'll say, "Adultery is stupid." I will not condone it even for other people.

Paul and I sit at our square mahogany dining room table. We have a microphone between us, and a very smart journalist named Alice Lake has pulled a long list of questions from her briefcase. She tells us the article will appear in May. As we chat, I am struck by the fact that over the five years of our marriage Paul has perfected his "rap" and transmogrified into the "perfect husband." I draw a deep breath, wondering why he irritates me. Maybe it's because he is once again the best in the class—only this time the class of spouses present consists of the two of us. He speaks as though his understanding of our marital situation is deeper than mine. His eagerness to explain and philosophize is more energetic, and his whole deportment is as though he's at a spelling bee. While I keep apologizing, saying that he's smarter than I, he makes it clear that any ordinary man could not live with a woman with my temper, my ambition, and my demands.

INTERVIEWER: What made you leave New Haven, where Paul apparently had a promising academic career at Yale?

SUSAN: I was just obsessed with getting to New York. The last year in New Haven I was already getting to do the kind of professional journalism I wanted to, but the magazines were in New York. I felt very trapped in New Haven. Paul was very amenable about it. He wanted to come as much as I.

PAUL: Well, there was a clash. I think I would have stayed in New Haven. I started thinking about leaving because of arguments that we had about no future for Susan and being depressed and all that kind of stuff. But I think my career moved more quickly here than it would have at Yale.

(Why, I wonder, is Paul saying there was a clash? And I stammer and rush into an apology for having been selfish. I am learning in front of a stranger that he was—and is—angry at me. I feel a physical twinge of fear.)

SUSAN: The pace is different here, Paul does many more things that I don't think he would have done if he'd stayed in the elitest academic atmosphere. I must say I felt very guilty about trying to come to New York when I felt that Paul would probably be much more comfortable in New Haven. After covering consciousness-raising meetings as a reporter, I understood the feelings better. I'm not saying they dissipated completely, but I understand them better. It wasn't just my problem."

(I feel shame confiding to this woman that I was the sort of wife who would ask her husband to relocate because of her career. Paul and I both know the move was primarily for me. But he never objected. He said that I was right as I cried late one night while we lay in bed—that he too would be enriched leaving New Haven and coming to New York. He agreed that Yale might find him more desirable later on if he left for a few years. But now he says he remembers arguments. Maybe

Paul is beginning to think his way out of our mutual marital myth. Is he revising our story to imply I made spoiled, selfish demands? I have never heard him talk like this before about the "perfect couple."

For so many of our friends we are the "perfect couple." Late-night whispered compliments after parties include: "You and Paul give us the last hope, my girl friend and me, that we can be happy . . ." When I confided this, unsure if I were bragging, to a newly divorced friend, she laughed at me. "Every couple is the perfect couple, dummy, until they split. Do you know how many people laid that trip on my husband and me? Sometimes I think our fans were our major reason we stayed together. We liked the portrait people drew of us. Every marriage breakup has a Greek chorus of crying friends who ask, 'But how could they, they are the perfect couple.' "

Perhaps Paul had felt resentment all along and had been afraid to articulate it. I don't know. But today, revisionism has entered our "happy home." As the reporter decorously but firmly examines us, I begin to see the reshaping of the myths we created together. When I talk to divorced or divorcing people, I notice that they give cold-blooded accounts of the relationship they've left behind. "I married her because we both played tennis and I wanted to get a place where I could sleep with a woman out of my parents' house." Or, "I married him because I felt lonely in graduate school." I do believe that these statements are the opposite of the blissful illusion that everybody was desperately trying to fit the data of his or her imperfect relationship into while the blush was still on the rose. The final stage of the revisionist process demotes the former relationship to one of neurosis. "We fell in together because I was such a weakling and yet felt so ambitious, I knew I needed a strong, successful man."

I, too, seem to have new angry feelings. It is hard for me to sort them out. Paul is the person I love. I can feel that feeling, both in memory and in the moment. Yet, as I am standing more and more on my feet, as I am feeling pride in my work, he is getting restless, demanding praise from our interviewer, and acting competitive. In short, we are becoming more equal, and as an emerging equal, I displease him. Feeling his resentment, I'm angry, yet I worry that I am hogging the spotlight in an unwifely manner. I feel selfish. I read somewhere that affairs are a way of getting back at a spouse. Maybe my anger has been developing for a while.)

INTERVIEWER: Which of you makes the most money?
PAUL: I make slightly more, or do you think you make more now?
SUSAN: No, I think it's almost equal now.

(I make more money currently. Why am I afraid to contradict him? I think Paul has brought in more money over the years.)

PAUL: It's started to move more to Susan right now. I think next year you'll probably make more.

(He's taken some of the burden of saying I make more money, thank God, the emasculating words didn't have to come from me.)

INTERVIEWER: Will that bother either of you?
SUSAN: No, I always feel that if you're doing what you want to do, it doesn't really matter. If by chance I happen to make more money—well, he's given me the chance to make money by moving to New York.
PAUL: I got an offer from another university at almost twice the salary. I felt a little freer to stay at N.Y.U.—which I preferred—because Susan was making money and I didn't have to worry about making more.

(What he has said is fair, generous. But as I watch Paul's familiar, ingratiating smile, his surges of energetic conversation, I feel confused. Why wouldn't he say I make more money now? Do I threaten him? Exactly. He is in competition with me. And to my surprise I'm in competition with him. I watch him exchange smiles with Alice Lake. He has just flashed his shy, lopsided grin. Of course he's the favorite here. He's always our conversation-setter and the social charmer.)

INTERVIEWER: Suppose Susan is wildly successful. Do you think it's going to be disturbing to either of you?

As I shake my head no, he answers.

PAUL: Well, I think—I'm sure I'd be slightly jealous, a little bit. But proud. I feel I'd be very hypocritical if it really meant very much to me. Because I've wanted her to do stuff like that, and I've encouraged her to do it. I would hope that pride would overcome jealousy.

(But he's never said he'd be jealous before. This feels to me like a careful statement of competition. Paul is staging a confrontation with this woman as referee. Maybe he's never talked to me like this because we're not close anymore. But, as the interviewer progresses, I bend over backward to play the adoring, slightly inferior wife.)

INTERVIEWER: Do you think of one or the other as head of the family, the way the census form asked for "head of the family" and then "wife"?

SUSAN: (speaking in my adult business voice and wondering if Paul resents my pomposity the way I resent his ingratiating charm) I think of it that way. The whole superiority thing of the male. I think that's very important to people when they marry. I really do. I have a feeling that the man is the head of the family. What I did was to marry a man who, I knew, was smarter than I am. Because that's what I value—brains. I guess you want to be dominated in some way.

(I sound awful. Am I a feminist or not? Am I going to see both sides of every question so I paralyze myself for the rest of my life? Is my response real, or am I contriving to present myself as a weak person? Well, remember my mother will read this interview. And I am a good daughter. I remember her ominous silences after I'd ask, "Suppose I don't get married, then what?" or "Why doesn't Uncle George help around the kitchen?"

I am describing a reality to Alice Lake. Maybe it's a past reality though. When I fell for Paul I wanted to capture the best and brightest man I knew. He was my trophy. In the years that followed, he was to become my emotional support and I his. But in the beginning there was the trophy.)

INTERVIEWER: Do you plan to have children?
SUSAN: Eventually. I'm not too excited by it now.

(Am I simply a spoiled brat? That's what my mother would say. A feminist wife would be defined as a bad wife by almost every adult I grew up respecting.)

PAUL: I'm interested in it. I think we go through periods of wanting to more than other times.
INTERVIEWER: Do you think your problems will become more complex then?
SUSAN: (Again I speak in my formal voice and try to give the impression that this reasonable speech I've memorized to gloss over the panic at the idea of children is true. Maybe I should start tallying up the half-lies I'm telling in this interview.) Oh, yes. You have this terrific desire to watch the child changing and developing, and on the other hand you still want to continue with what was very gratifying before. Your work might seem less important—I have the fear it might suddenly get less important. I'm not sure that I'd like that. You don't know yourself until you have a child, you don't know that you're going to develop these feelings of maternity.

(I feel hypocritical. If only I'd said what I thought, that I've occasionally had doubts about sharing parenthood with Paul.

I resent his patriarchal and sometimes patronizing uneasiness with children. Though I myself often shifted from foot to foot wondering what to say to friends' kids who appeared to be doing fine without my hellos or good-byes. An occasional child squeezing onto my lap or volunteering a good-bye kiss has both unnerved and moved me.

I remember when Paul and I were in college we saw silent home movies at his parents' house of Paul as a baby at the seashore. My throat tightened as I watched the beautiful little child with the dark hair, sensual lips, and almond-shaped eyes playing by the ocean. I yearned for a child like that then. But now I have become distracted. For years Paul has said he wants children, but lately he hasn't been so insistent. New York is a playground for adults. In New Haven we saw Paul's friends who talked about history—shoptalk that seemed monotonous and left me out. New Yorkers talk with people who are not in their fields. They go to new restaurants, movies, and theater. Children become a financial burden in a city where apartment space is expensive and private schools seem more of a necessity than an indulgence to the upwardly mobile.

I had read books and books extolling the virtues of procreation, starting with Plato's theory that immortality comes only through one's children. I vaguely put off the blessed event, saying, "Oh, someday," and comforted myself for my lack of interest with the words of a male friend, a colleague of Paul's at Yale, who had once told me that becoming a father had been one of the most moving experiences of adult life. He had felt a completed adult; but the appearance of his first baby had brought unexpected and tender feelings of paternity—he felt emotionally grown. I vaguely assumed this would happen to me. Having a baby seemed the same as getting married. If you listened to people like your parents you would automatically give birth. As long as you pretended not to hear them, there was no reason to do it.

I am bossy and scared. I want some things my way and

am afraid to speak out for them. I married Paul prepared to adore his mind, his restless quest for obscure facts, for inventing abstract theories about history and movies. But I refused to agree when he'd start fantasizing that he'd teach his child Greek by the time he was three, like John Stuart Mill. "Mill had a nervous breakdown," I'd say, hoping I would not have to witness a young mind being force-fed like a goose.

Now I desperately want this interview to end. I can't stop thinking that I am lying; me, one half of this "perfect couple."

I won't tell our inquisitor that I read a psychology book that said the well-adjusted male in this country is aggressive, ambitious, and wants to order his own life, while the well-adjusted female is passive, childish, and desires to please one other person, that is, her husband. When I married Paul I had done what every female teen-ager dreams about. Prince Charming didn't ride a white horse but rather was emotionally supportive, won poetry contests and honors in college, and knew about the pathetic fallacy and divine right of kings, and how to break up conversation with outlandish wit. But for me, it turned out, this was not enough. In fact his Prince Charmingness often undermined my own sense of self-worth. I didn't just want to be the hanger-on to a successful person, I wanted to experience some success myself. I felt more diminished and miserable when I went to parties with the successful academics that Paul knew. And right now my playing second fiddle to his decent, intellectually sound, perfect-husband solo act is driving me crazy. Why haven't I felt this way before? What is going on?)

INTERVIEWER: Paul, what's good for you about your wife having a career?
PAUL: Well, I think it makes me feel very uneasy to be depended on. I like to be the strong one in a lot of situations. But I somehow find it so much more satisfying that Susan has work to do and is interested in it. I'm just thinking back to

New Haven when she hated the kind of life we had and the kind of abrasions and disruptions and what have you. This is so much better. We do have conflicts. One is that Susan is out a lot meeting people during the day and when she comes home she doesn't especially want to see people. I'm in my office and I'm teaching and things like that, and sometimes at night I want to go out.

(I am angry at his turning the woman's positive question again into a criticism of our relationship. She'd asked him what was good about my having a career and he built in the negative answer. Maybe I look at him too closely, I think, avoiding his eyes, pretending we are two panel members on a talk show. I can't believe that I ever heard him speak so coldly about me. I shiver and feel like I want to crawl under the bedclothes. I don't like this dual look at our marital bond.)

SUSAN: You see, I don't like to be very social. When I think about relaxing, I think about being by myself. Paul, when he thinks about relaxing, thinks about having a party or going to a party. I'm just surprised at the number of women who work hard and also work at entertaining. It's very hard for me. (There I am apologizing again, saying that maybe some superwoman could do it, but I can't. Why am I thinking one thing and saying something else?)
PAUL: That's one place where I get resentful sometimes, that Susan doesn't want to entertain, or when there's some faculty party that she doesn't want to go to. I have to go by myself or make excuses or not go at all. There's a sense in which I would want her ideally to be a consort, to come to parties and that kind of thing.

(I am dying to push my chair away from the table and walk out. Paul has again emphasized his resentment. I look at him smiling at the interviewer. It's quite clear to me that the two of them are getting on famously, while I'm exhausted by my efforts to analyze my confusion. But I am determined to keep smiling.

INTERVIEWER: And Susan, the pluses for you about having a career?
SUSAN: I am very proud that I make some money of my own, but basically you have the sense that the husband is the bread-winner, and the outside world looks at you that way. I don't think everything's one hundred percent, you know. I feel his work is more important than mine in some sense. I think that being a journalist is less important to the eternal verities than being an academic.

(I am demeaning myself, hoping that Paul will come through with a proud plug for the little woman.)

PAUL: It seems like there could be two theories of marriage: one, a kind of complementary theory, like everything I can't do, you do, and vice versa. And another kind of dual theory: there are two people, each of whom does everything. The more traditional marriage is a complementary one—there are certain things that the wife does and there are certain things that the husband does. Some things are masculine, and some things are feminine. And really in a kind of day-to-day way, it strengthens the idea that men and women really are two different species that can't possibly communicate with each other just because they live in such completely different spheres. So if there's a movement from one kind of marriage to another, it should be a very good thing. Many men still think they're getting a lot of benefits out of marrying a passive woman. I think they could get a lot more from a woman with her own identity.

Paul has pulled it off. He has provided an intellectual ideology for the perfect couple. Yet in the interview both of us have put me down as causing conflicts, either because I

wanted to be in New York (read unfeminine ambition) or because I won't go to enough parties with him. And I have put
myself down as doing work inferior to his, and I—who have
felt rage, jealousy, and guilt during the interview—have ex-
pressed none of it. And to pin the tail on the interview, Paul
has spun out the theoretical base for our union. It's the old
story of the supercompetent man, the bar-mitzvah boy who
made good, and the weak, selfish bitch. If this is the perfect
couple—where am I?

Paul and Alice Lake stand up, the interview mercifully
over, and they stretch their arms above their heads, then grin
at each other, and at me. Neither notices my uneasiness.

I suddenly remember Jim St. Clare. Does every model
marriage include infidelity? I doubt it.

Paul follows her out into the hallway elaborating his anti-
complementary theory of marriage with a semiflirtatious smile
on his face, his eyes flashing with good humor. Why am I so
sure that he has done well in the interview and I have flubbed?
Tonight I will skip dinner and try to blot out the afternoon in
sleep. After all, nothing is wrong. Nothing is wrong unless
I think it is, and I think nothing is wrong.

FEBRUARY

February 6

Late last night, long after we'd switched off our reading lamps, I put my cheek tenderly against Paul's shoulder while he was lying on his stomach, and whispered, "I love you, dear, but you're a stranger to me." I've said this to him many times. As usual he lay quietly for a moment and then answered, his words muffled by the pillow, "I love you, too."

"You're a stranger to me," I whispered again, teasing but asking for something, what I couldn't say. I yearned to know him better, yet I was also saying that I am becoming a stranger to him. Maybe I wanted him to draw me out, make me confess about Jim St. Clare. What would I confess? I don't miss him. I remind myself that the experience was a little like catching a cold. It makes you feel uncomfortable for a while, but the symptoms disappear and you're back to normal. Still, I couldn't tell Paul that I have slept with another man; I can't expect him to reassure me about everything.

One night he scared me by answering, "Yes, I am a stranger. I have secrets you'll never know," but refused to tell me what he meant. After pleading with him for an hour, I carried my pillow into the living room to sleep on the couch.

A dramatic move that felt a little silly. I kept waking up, expecting him to come and tell me to come back to bed, that the conversation had been meaningless. During the night a half-remembered Sherwood Anderson line popped into my head: "Even in Winesburg, Ohio, people live and die alone." And I cried myself back to sleep. Last night was different. "Strangers?" Paul said. "That's why we love each other, because we have mysteries. If there were no spaces between us, there'd be no room for our love either."

MARCH

March 10

Yesterday I telephoned John Schwartz, the rock music critic, to ask if I could interview him. A woman at *Glamour* told me recently that she had met him at a midnight concert and he'd been calling her to discuss the Beatles and the American jazz tradition. I had a twitch of envy of her and her single life as she told her story. I've admired Schwartz's writing for a long time. So when my *New York Times* editor asked me to add a little historical analysis to my article on James Taylor, I had a good excuse to call Schwartz.

"Yeah," he said. "Well, come over now, doll. I'm free for a few hours." I was taken aback by his abruptness. I felt unprepared, though I've spent weeks thinking about the piece. As I hung up the telephone, I told Paul I was going out to interview Schwartz. "Why see him?" he asked. "That's crazy. You and I can work out some paragraphs ourselves. I tell you, you don't need him." I was surprised. I used to take Paul's advice as law on my articles. He always reads them over when I'm finished. But I can and do work out my own paragraphs. I knew he was wrong. So I ignored his tirade and concentrated on what I knew was going to be an interesting morning.

I took a cab over to the East River where the sun seems to shine a little brighter on the cleaner windows and trimmer facades of the tall buildings. I was shocked when Schwartz opened his door. I guess I expected to see someone my own age. He looked like a chic elder statesman, with long brown hair, thick sideburns, and smoky gray aviator glasses. He glared at me, then lowered his eyes and motioned me in. I sat down on a black suede couch, rubbing my palms on my dungarees and admiring a decor that consisted mostly of silver and black stripes and eight-feet-high speakers.

I took out my notebook and fumbled in the bottom of my pocketbook for a pencil while he leapt from his seat and disappeared into his kitchen. I heard a refrigerator door slam and he yelled in, "D'you want a drink? Liquor gets me going." As he bounced back into the room I noticed his Gucci shoes and skin-tight silk shirt wildly decorated with rosebuds. Nobody in New Haven wore silk shirts with rosebuds. I silently admired the vanity that made him dress like a rock musician rather than the bookish college professor I knew he once was. He watched me intently as I phrased my first question about soft-rock music. When he began to answer, I hunched over my notebook, avoiding the brown eyes.

During a pause, he jumped up to refill his Scotch glass. I followed him into the kitchen and while he mixed his drink with slow precision, I blurted out, "I've always admired your writing. When I was wishing I was a reporter, I used to say I'd give anything to write like you, like that piece of yours on the Motown empire. I thought that was great."

He didn't turn around, but he thanked me in his testy voice. As we walked back into the living room he asked me what I'd written about. I didn't mention Jim St. Clare because I didn't feel like facing Schwartz's questions. I sat down again on the suede couch, squirming for a comfortable position, and went on: "Why can't rich white kids sing the blues?" After about a half hour I realized that I knew more about James

Taylor's music than he did. Just as I began to wonder if in fact Paul had been right, he jumped to his feet and put a James Taylor record on his machine and began to describe notes, chords, and rhythms. "You are smart," he said, cleaning the needle. "You know a lot about the kid, maybe I can tell you about the music." He made me hear the music as if it were the first time, and finished by singing along with two bars of syncopated percussion. When the record was over, he rushed to lift the needle. The room, which had been pulsating moments before with the sound of the giant speakers and his staccato voice, was silent.

I opened my mouth to speak, but before I could he'd bounded to the couch and was stroking my hair murmuring, "You have the silkiest furs in the world. Your hair is like silky fur." I was scared. Maybe Jim's behavior wasn't so weird. People in the music business must make a lot of passes at women. My mind raced along. Funny I haven't thought about Jim very much for over a month until now. Maybe it's me, though. Maybe I'm giving men cues that I'm open. No.

"No, no, this isn't what I came for," I said, pushing against his unmoving body. "Well, you got what you came for, now try this. I am not a bad person," he answered. "No," I stood swaying on my feet, smoothing my hair in an effort to reclaim it, "I have to go now." "Well," and now he wasn't looking at me, "I'm sorry to upset you. Let me read you something I wrote about jazz before you go."

His voice had lost its urgent appeal and I had lost his eyes. "No, I have to go, I tell you," I said desperately, but also sensing that my desperation was unnecessary, that I had broken the contact between us. I felt let down and found myself muttering my thanks while I gathered my coat and searched for my notebook, which I had been sitting on. "Okay," he said, "nice to meet you." He sounded obedient, ashamed. "It was good talking to you, yes, because I gotta give a lecture on this stuff tomorrow afternoon at N.Y.U."

And with his head down, he walked quietly to the door and opened it; he nodded as we shook hands, looking somewhere to my right, and I swept out to the elevator.

On the way home I replayed our conversation, congratulating myself on my professionalism, on my questions, and the fact that I was able to sound intelligent. And Schwartz had liked me. I'll go to sleep now, but I won't eat dinner. And tomorrow I'll go to his lecture.

March 11: Afternoon

Today I went to Memorial Hall at N.Y.U. I wondered what he would do when he saw me. I hoped he wouldn't be angry that I'd come. One student tried to strike up a conversation with me. "Are you a friend of Dr. Schwartz's? Yeah? Well, if you happen to know his phone number, maybe you could call him. He's a half hour late. Wait, here he comes, never mind."

Standing in front of a giant multicolored globe, he was wearing a salmon-colored suit, fitted and shoulder-padded, with a baby blue scarf. He pulled the chair away from the table and started to fiddle with his tape recorder, then glanced over and saw me. I moved my lips into a formal smile, but he seemed not to notice.

But his lecture or nonstop acoustical tirade was great. I kept admiring his references to Greek myths, his put-downs of stultifying attitudes while demonstrating his own classical background. He also drew the kids out—talking to them like equals and making them feel they had interesting things to say. At the end of his talk, he giggled his strange high-pitched titter, and then walked over to touch the giant globe with his fingertips as though he were a magician. "We've done it, people, and we've done it together in the world room. Ladies and

Gentlemen, this has been Professor John Schwartz live from the world room." This seemed a delightfully irreverent and mockingly egocentric statement, and the students burst into applause. Instead of an arms-high gesture, he shrugged and shuffled back to the table to turn off his tape recorder and to face the questions of the students.

As the students started filing out, I wondered what I would do. How would he approach me here on the field of his recent performance? He ignored me. I found myself trailing behind him and an entourage that included several students, a few sophisticated-looking New York women, and a fatuous male dean. "Hi," I called, squirming between two young boys who were repeating a pun John Schwartz had made. "I'd like to check a few quotes with you," I explained, hanging in, matching his quick pace as the group began to disappear out into the night through a series of swinging doors. "Don't bother," he looked at me fearfully through the thick aviator glasses, "I trust you. Just spell my name right. How'd you hear about this lecture, anyway?" he whispered as everybody else was concentrating on getting through the doors. "You told me yesterday," I explained, lowering my eyes nervously. "Yeah, well groovy," he said loudly. "See you soon, doll, and don't sweat the quotes." "Yes, but I mean I'm quoting you as somebody I disagree with. Maybe you just want to check . . ." "Just cool it." He waved grandly and then I was alone in the hallway in the classroom building, surrounded by elevator signs, marble floors, and oil paintings of dead teachers.

I was unable to tell if I was disappointed or relieved that I had not been picked up tonight by the whirlwind I now knew I was stalking. I was jealous of the happy group that had disappeared into the night with their laughter and mysterious cohesion; yet there was something about the look in his eyes when he spoke to me, a terror and fascination that assured me we had not seen the last of each other. I was elated. It was like a feeling I'd once had in college after taking Dexamil for an exam. My legs walked automatically in double time, I wasn't even aware that I had left the building to walk across a darkened busy street. I found myself humming as I unlocked my front door without remembering how I'd got home.

March 11: Evening

Paul has made me an all-vegetable dinner since we're both dieting. While we eat I tell about the lecture. Confessing my admiration gives me a way to get rid of some of my guilt. He listens in silence and nods a few times and tries to disagree or modify a few points.

I am in such a whirl, I find it hard to hear him. I am then stricken and go over to Paul and hug him as he's eating. He puts his arm up and pats me without turning around. Why doesn't he woo me, stare at me, or even look at me anymore? "C'mon," I tease, "give me a full hug." "I like it when you hug me," he says, pursing his lips in a happy pout. "I like it when you hug me."

March 16

I bicycled across the park this afternoon and observed New Yorkers walking dogs, necking, picnicking, and strolling in the first warm spring day. I rode up and down Schwartz's street and looked at the river for a while and then walked my bike into the coffee shop on his corner, wondering if he'd happen by. I was behaving strangely. I watched the people leaving his apartment building. It is as if I were contemplating a move into the neighborhood.

It's early evening when I finally get back home; Paul is reading some student papers at our dining room table where we often work together. I enjoy working while he works. We are not lonely and yet we are each doing what we enjoy. Today, however, he is working alone. When the telephone rings, he answers it, and looks slightly distracted and hangs up immediately. "What was that?" I ask, wandering over to my typewriter. "Wrong number," says Paul without looking at me. There's something in his silence that gives me pause. Could John Schwartz be calling and then . . . no, impossible, I think, shocked that I would even think about an adult doing something so childish.

When Paul disappears to pick up the laundry in the basement a few minutes later, the telephone rings again. I answer it, to hear John's dry voice, "Howya doin', dear? You're a hard person to pin down." "Was that you calling before?" I ask stiffly. "Waddya expect? How the hell else am I supposed to find you?" he answers. "I don't like hanging up on people, but I don't know your scene and I wanted to talk to you. And I don't want to make trouble."

My silence indicates my confused reactions, and he continues talking to fill the space. I am shocked and excited to hear from him, but I am not sure why. "Ahh, well, I'd like to get together and shoot the breeze if you want," he is saying. "Whatdaya say, Monday a week? I'm scheduled to go to California for a week tonight. I got an idea for an article I think you could help me on." I am mollified, flattered that he would be interested in a discussion with me. But I am not sure I want to pick up the threads that would lead me back into his apartment. "Okay," I say hoarsely. "Okay," clearing my throat. "Monday afternoon about four, okay?"

I am attaching too much symbolic importance to Paul's moods. When he returns with the laundry, I study his face. "Let's do something fun tonight," I suggest. "Oh, okay, but I'd just as soon work," he answers, disappearing into the bed-

room. I am crestfallen. Okay, if that's the way he wants it. I'll
arrange my own fun. I know I am looking for ways to make
myself feel less the villain, the heavy.

March 18

Sunday morning and Paul is acting restless. He paces into
the living room where I am flipping across the bright-colored
ads in the *Times* spring fashions for women.

"I want to go to the Brooklyn Museum. There's a great
exhibit of nineteenth-century French lithographs there," he
announces. "But I don't feel like going alone." I hate to go to
museums. I was overexposed to them as a child and feel
tired after walking for about ten minutes. I always feel as
though I am under someone's pedagogical strictures as I dutifully follow the other seers around the floor. Sometimes I watch
a fellow watcher or eavesdrop on a conversation to ease the
boredom. Adults who are married to each other should be
able to go places without each other, I tell myself. I can turn
him down if I don't feel like accompanying him. But I feel
sorry for Paul as he answers, as I knew he would, "I don't
feel like going alone. It makes me sad."

"Why not ask Tim to go with you?" He is pulling on his
curly hair with one hand and holding his ever-present book
open against his body with the other palm. I watch him and
wonder what he is really thinking about.

"Hummm," I repeat. "Why not ask your friend Tim?"
Tim is his best friend from college who now teaches at John
Jay Police Academy. Tim always seems very attached to Paul:
he called us in New Haven when his brother died; but Paul's
attachment has never been clear to me. "I don't know. Anyway, he's away this week." "Okay," I stand up and stretch.
Sundays are a time for standing up and stretching and then

falling back into chairs or onto sofas or even into beds again, in my opinion. "We'll think of somebody for you to ask out on a museum date." Paul smiles and sits down on a chair. "I know," I say triumphantly. "Why not ask Emily?"

We've been going to these parties with three or four couples about six years older than we are who live in big upper West Side apartments. Of the four couples crucial to this crowd, Emily and Arthur are the most social. Southerners, and each on their second marriage, Arthur is an Episcopal priest and Emily is an empathetic red-headed woman who teaches photography part-time in a private school. Paul, who knows they bore me, has been urging me to invite them over for dinner, but I've ducked the question. He finds them interesting because they've done some group sex and taken a few acid trips. They are the sort of couple that Paul would enjoy substituting for our married friends in New Haven. It's nothing I can put my finger on, but when they earnestly begin to describe how doorways turned colors while they were acid tripping, or question me about people I've interviewed, I answer by rote without challenge or added insight from them.

I have enjoyed their dinner parties where Emily seems effortlessly to produce huge earthenware trays (made by her first husband, she whispers to me) covered with fried Japanese-style shrimp and carrots from a warm kitchen stocked with everything from soybean sprouts to home-grown sorrel. Arthur is a bit withdrawn, as Emily explains to everyone who comes to her parties. And everyone smiles with relief that it isn't their fault that Arthur prefers to sit by himself on a couch stroking Morris, their black cat. But Paul likes Arthur, as much as he likes Emily, he says, and he often seeks Arthur's opinions on subjects like the differences between American and English Episcopalians, much to Arthur's surprise and gentle pleasure.

"Why *not* ask Emily?" Paul smiles. "That's a really good idea." As his voice rises with enthusiasm, he asks, "She probably won't want to go, will she?" "No, I bet she will be pleased to go," I answer. "If she hasn't already seen the exhibit. And you could probably learn a few things. She's a photographer, she's got the eye to see things in pictures that we can't."

Paul has already disappeared to the telephone to call her, but then he returns a few seconds later. "I don't know," he says. "Look, I'll call her," I announce. As a journalist I have learned to have few second thoughts between my impulse and the actual dialing of the telephone. It is one area where I've managed to lose my ambivalence. I dial, grateful for the opportunity to assert my goodwill toward Emily without having to invest my own time. "Hello Emily," and then I make a speech about how Paul wants to go to the exhibit and how I thought perhaps she'd enjoy seeing it and helping him see new facets of the art, so please why didn't she speak to him? In three minutes it is done. She will pick him up in her station wagon and they'll drive to Brooklyn today. He disappears to change his shirt, and I smile to myself because I have been able to find this Solon-like solution—and to think in years gone by that I'd have been nervous or jealous to send him off like this with another woman.

March 20

Parties often disappoint me. In my teens, as I combed my hair and put in my contact lenses, I hoped that someone like Paul would be there to drawl caustically about my new dungaree skirt or recommend some bit of esoterica, a book like *Punch* magazine's cartoons of World War II, or Turin's pornography. But these days I meet enough new people as a reporter.

Paul has developed a passion for parties with this boring

group of married couples including Emily and Arthur and refuses to go alone. "How would it look? And besides, I get lonely if you're not there."

So tonight I put on my purple leotard and step into my purple jeans. I don't want to spend my evening making superficial chitchat with semi-strangers, even though they are gracious hosts. Maybe I am jealous of Paul's enthusiasm for these people. As we enter the sprawling Riverside Drive building, he rushes ahead of me into the self-service elevator. Upstairs the elevator lurches to a halt and in the dim corridor we hear the uneven sounds of talk and laughter.

I smile at Emily, our hostess, and compliment her on the beige velvet jumpsuit she's wearing. Paul's head whirls around and he too eyes her in the clinging suit. "Very nice," he grins sheepishly. In fact she and I had gone together to look at clothes one day and I had urged her to purchase the suit. As I look at her in it more closely, I wonder sourly if it was such a great idea, since her stomach sticks out in it like a baby's in Dr. Denton pajamas. Paul disappears into the crowd and is soon the center of a small group by the long spread of windows overlooking Riverside Drive and the park.

I watch my husband agree to roll a joint with our hostess. I hear him excitedly telling her about an article he thinks I should write. Then I am contrite now about my reluctance to be here. But I am bored. Jim has been gone for six months, and I miss the excitement of rushing out to his late-night concerts. Alfred, a lonely, lecherous husband, whispers startlingly in my ear, though at a party it's unfair to define intrusive behavior, "You just had a nice thought, didn't you?"

I mumble something, feeling stupid; I look away to see Charlotte Winston come in to the party by herself. I make my way through the mixture of upper West Side professionals and their wives to her side. She's a contemporary of the hostess. Both are Southerners and seem very exotic to me. They are also both about eight years my senior and I sometimes get a kick out of listening to Charlotte drop worldly-wise comments about life and love. Recently she winked a blue eye at me and cooed, "I just don't know a thing about you and your marriage, Susan. I just know that first marriages are not made for sex or money. They're made for love and emotional security. Don't say a word, not a word . . ." I, of course, said nothing, but felt astounded at the wisdom that would have a category and a definition of something that was my whole life.

Now Charlotte and I observe the revelers with some complicity. She is drinking gin and tonic, and her white silk turban is slightly askew. She almost gets away with the effect.

She gracefully lowers herself onto a leather ottoman, surveys the large living room bounded by our hostess's huge photographs of wildflowers, and then murmurs softly, "Awful boring I expect, Susan?" Her voice tinkles and oversyllabizes with Southern seductiveness and, relieved to have somebody corroborate my own lack of interest in the group, I nod.

"What is the reason for these parties?" Charlotte is looking casually into her nearly empty gin and tonic, and poking lazily at her turban. "Why are these parties held week after week?" she asks, much in the same manner that a teacher starts a long lecture. "I'll tell you why. Somebody wants to convene these deadly folks for secret meetings with somebody else."

My throat gets tight. Could she be right? Why do Paul and I have a perpetual fight lately that reaches a pitch on Friday nights when he announces that Emily and Arthur are having a get-together on Saturday night and he'd said we could go. After our Saturday-night dinner I long to sit down in front of my typewriter for an hour, breaking only for a banal situation comedy to clear my head and then again for a late-night walk with Paul. I also love to go to the movies with him. We hold hands in the dark and predict murders or seduction scenes. He is the only person I know who likes to talk at the movies besides me.

But lately when I say, "Those parties are boring, and we just saw everybody last Saturday night," he looks at me as though I am the sole obstacle between him and pleasure. "You're such a hermit," he accuses. "Those people like you. You're just afraid to make new friends. And once you get there you'll have a good time." Once I get there I do not have a good time. I simply don't have a bad time.

I smile insincerely at Charlotte, and suddenly both our heads turn toward a conversation taking place on a huge fat sofa on the other side of the long white living room. There has been an explosion of laughter. We peer at the group, and someone moves away, exposing the interior of the cluster where Paul sits on a plump ottoman with his elbows on his knees. Our hostess is sitting between his legs on the floor, her laughing face stretched up to his, her neck taut with the strain. Now she leans her head back against the inside of his thigh in exhausted merriment. My nerves twitch violently as though she had hit me with the contact she made with my husband. And I think I understand something of why she calls me during the week to make casual conversation. She has a crush on my husband. Almost as though I'd spoken out loud, I hear her friend Ann standing above her say, "Well, if I had to pick the perfect husband I'd pick Paul."

My nerves leap again. I think there's something terribly private about the husbandness of Paul; only *I* can experience it. I feel these sophisticated women, who talk of first marriages, rating husbands, and extramarital affairs, are dancing casually over points of my privacy that become impulses of pain for me when they are exposed. But what about you, hypocrite? I ask myself. You have no right to begrudge Paul any flirtation or even affair (the word sounds awful) after the way you carried on with Jim.

I strain to see Paul's face, but he is hidden by the crowd around him. As Charlotte raises an eyebrow without looking at my face and flashes her dimples in a look of concern, I wend my way through the other guests to stand behind him. I put my hands on his shoulders, conscious that a look of tension passes over the hostess's vulnerable face. He quickly leaps to his feet and we clutch hands in our silly way that we do when we're first meeting after a few hours' separation. "Are you tired, honey?" he asks sweetly. "Are you having fun?" Assuaged by the fact that I can so easily pull him from the group, my nerves feel calmer. I look at him with warmth. He is my husband, even if we don't discuss it much any more. "Come over here and talk to me for a while," I whisper, and still holding hands we walk together to the window. The hostess watches us sharply or is it my imagination, my adolescent fantasy that my husband is attractive to all women? Suddenly she rises to disappear for the evening into her bedroom.

March 23

A week has gone by, and I keep changing my mind about meeting with John Schwartz. I'm afraid I'm asking for trouble, but I want to go. Just the idea makes me smile as I squeeze into the crowded Broadway bus in the early evening. But if I go I will be taking something away from my relationship with Paul.

My psychiatrist asks me if seeing Schwartz will make me meaner or nicer to Paul when I'm with him. "Nicer," I respond. I know that I would resent Paul for having made me deny myself the pleasure.

But this morning, Monday, as Paul gets out of bed and disappears into the kitchen, I am convinced that I won't keep the appointment.

So at the office I dial Schwartz's telephone number, feeling my most formal voice about to explain that pressures of article deadlines make this meeting an impossibility. As the telephone rings I imagine the possibilities: He's at the movies and will return later; I've misdialed; he's not answering because he's typing against his deadline. I redial. No answer. About three, I leave work and take a bus to his house. I am let down. My resolves have been irrelevant. The man had not even been interested enough to remember to break the appointment. At his doorstep I search for his name on the gold plates. I ring his bell belligerently. Then forlornly. Then I decide to leave a note. "Where were you? It's a lovely day today and I hope you're okay."

March 24

My telephone rings and he asks, "How're you doing, kid?" I am relieved. I am also hooked. "Where were you?" "Well, I kinda got tied up in California, hon, and I thought about calling you, but figured it would be cool if I didn't. I'm sorry. Whatcha doin' right now?" "Nothing." What I was doing was moping around the house, ignoring my typewriter and wondering if I should have gone with my husband to Rutgers where he was giving a guest lecture on Puritan sects. I am surprising myself because, when I do sit down at the typewriter, it's often to jot down random notes like this one about how addled and isolated I feel. He is still talking. "Well, I'd still like to talk to you. Could you lend me your James Taylor records? I've been thinking about dashing off a quickie on the subject. Our talk got me going."

I find myself agreeing to meet him at my house to give him my notes. But there's something akin to professional jealousy in my head as I prepare the pile for him. Taylor was my obsession for three months. For about four weekends I'd heard him in concerts from campuses to town halls across Pennsylvania, Ohio, and New York. I had stayed up late with him in his hotel room, smelled his socks sweaty and rotten from the inside of his old hiking boots, heard him calmly

answering 3:00 A.M. calls from hysterical adolescent fans,
watched him drink one Scotch after another hunched in the
corner of tawdry motel bars while he told me of his ideas on
love, drugs, and music and what combination of the three
makes his life worth living.

I feel that journalistically speaking Taylor was my idea
—mine. Schwartz is the bigger writer; an article by him might
scoop me. Nonetheless I prepare my little journalistic care
packet, reprimanding myself for professional selfishness.

When he enters my darkish foyer to pick me up, I am
startled to see him a real person and in my house. It is his
casual, "C'mon we're late" that makes him seem okay, like
someone I knew or could know.

At the hamburger restaurant on my corner he takes my
package without a glance at it, thanking me perfunctorily.
"How long you lived in this garbage pail?" he asks. "What?"
"I mean the West Side. Only people who want to be reminded
constantly of the existence of garbage live here. Shabby pro-
fessors, righteous psychiatrists, and a lot of earnest women."
Provoked, I argue that the East Side is falsely glamorous, that
it is nearly immoral to spend money to isolate yourself under
the facade of wealth over there. "Don't give me that 'it feels
good to feel bad' line, sweetie. I've been shlepping for a living
for twenty years on campuses and now in these fershluggener
magazines. I'm just trying to ease the pain."

During dessert, he asks me, "Have you always been—
God help us—faithful to your husband? Or have you tried a
little bit to live?" I tell him that of course I had been faithful
to Paul. Except for—and incredibly I find myself telling him
about Jim. When I finish, he says curiously, "So that's the
only time in six years of marriage that you strayed. Mazel tov.
You deserve an award." "You're crazy," I answer. "Most
married people are faithful." "Sweetie," his voice is tired,
"married men are the horniest men in the world. They're the
only men to whom random sex is forbidden. I can't speak
for women, because I never was a married woman, but my

experience with them is that they're wild for sexual adventure."

I realize he thinks I sound naive; not the reaction I'd expected to my sordid secret. "So," he continues, picking up my fingers and linking them with his so that our palms touch, "What do you want from me?" Shocked by the physical move as well as the question, I let him idly play with my fingers for a few seconds. As I pull my hand away, I lean forward across the table, and hear myself saying in a choked rush of words, "I admire your writing, I would love to write like you. I mean I want to be you."

I trail off, not sure if I sound too intense, or too superficial.

He barely reacts, but continues playing with my fingers. "Why don't you ask me what I want from you?" he asks idly. "What?" I ask obediently, still shaky from my revelation. "Well," he slowly draws out his words, "I want to put my penis inside you. I want to hug you. I want to kiss you." I pull my hand away. "And," he continues, "you could get to know me, see how a free-lance writer shleps along. We'd make a good team." "Out of the question," I say, shocked at the directness of his words and how they turn me on. "I'm married, and I couldn't bear the tension." He shrugs and downs his wine. "Couldn't we just be friends?" I ask, conscious that I am the only one talking. "Honey," he says, twisting in his chair to signal the waiter for our check, "I know what you're saying. But I'm forty-one and just a little bit old and just a little bit too tired to have a pretty young woman hanging around without any sexual relationship. Ten years ago, when my ego was in better shape, that would have been a different story, maybe."

As we leave the restaurant neither of us speaks. I am disappointed that my chance to see this man's life, to make friends with him, has fallen through. We walk to my apartment building in silence and he nods good-bye. I walk inside toward the elevator and think about what I'll feel entering my empty apartment in a few minutes, reduced again to a world inhabited by old unexciting friends. Halfway across my lobby, I say good-night to the elevator man sitting, his legs apart, on the uncomfortable fake Italian renaissance chair. Then I turn around and walk back.

He is still standing where I left him, his arm up for a cab that has just stopped. As he sees me walking toward him, he gets that admiring fearful look around his eyes. "I changed my mind," I say again in that strained, high-pitched, uncontrolled voice. He nods and we both duck into the cab, one of the few graceful acts connected to living in the streets of New York.

In the cab, we huddle silently in separate corners of the back seat. At his corner, we emerge and we walk to his lobby. When I take off my coat, he starts stroking my hair. To me the moment is a strain. I'd exhausted myself making the decision to go through with it. "Come," he says, "let's get in bed." I follow him into his tiny bedroom, decorated only by a bed, a typewriter table, and several file cabinets. The light is dim and I feel I am going through motions that are new to me. As we lie there he says, "Sometimes it's better the first time just to feel you're getting to know the other person, and not to have sex at all. What do you think?" He looks at me shyly and again I feel touched by how well he understands me, behind his sophisticated New York clothes and words. He's still wearing his glasses and his body looks vulnerable with its too-rounded shoulders and white skin. I feel better. This is not just another ordeal. I am having an adventure. And I am sure I want this adventure desperately. I hug him impulsively in the half-light from his street. This man could never replace my husband in my life, but he would sure be interesting. As he smiles shyly, looking me squarely in the eyes, I am filled with a light-headed guiltless sense that I will have few problems integrating him into my life. As we slowly begin to touch each other's bodies I think of how much I would like to tell my husband about this amazing new adventure I am having.

APRIL

April 7

For two weeks now I have been calling John Schwartz
or he's been calling me and we meet in the late afternoon.
Words, theories, anecdotes, our life stories pour out of us.
He confides that he's scared to write and prefers to tell his
anecdotes or perceptions to an understanding face with a tape
recorder running. I encourage him to talk out his pieces with
me, and feel pleased that I can be of some help, since Paul
refuses to take help from me on any of his projects.

Today John is in a pensive mood. As he whirls a glass
of bourbon and tinkles the ice cubes, we sit in a rare silence
as the afternoon's sun slowly disappears. "Do you love me?"
he asks. His voice is mocking to lighten the question. "Why
do you ask me that?" I answer, glad that we don't see each
other too clearly in the darkening room. "Well, what are you
making for dinner tonight?" he answers. "Pork roast." "I wish
you'd make me pork roasts." I am touched by his wistful
remarks, but I am also sure about what I think love is. "Do
you love me?" I ask him, being evasive again. "I'm really
incapable of it, I think," he answers, "but some people aren't.
And I think you are capable of it. You are a good person."

"I don't think love is something that happens when two people are attracted to each other. I am infatuated with you, but love is what I feel for my husband." He disappears into the kitchen to get more liquor and ice for his glass. When he returns he laughs shortly. "In other words, my dear, you believe in the philosophy that in order to be in love you've got to be married or mated for eternity, you've got to feel trapped, isolated, frustrated, and horny. Why is it that most women decide they want to get married when lust leaves a relationship? It's probably then they feel secure, more in control."

It is at times like this that I am struck by the unlived portions of my life. If my wedding was meant to be a perfect ending to a love story, then of course the marriage went largely unexamined. I still feel uneasy speaking about my husband to people, including my psychiatrist, because I feel it is a betrayal. John Schwartz startles me with his cynicism and wisdom—a result of twenty or twenty-five years of looking through other people's and his own illusions. I am struck dumb by the way he refutes my romantic ideas. I also am learning that behind his bark is a gentleness and timidity. As I am memorizing him, he is trying to understand and be kind to me.

"But I am so afraid to be alone," I'd murmur after he'd complete a monologue about how death is waking up next to the same person for forty years every morning. "C'mon, honey," he'd snap, "Unmarried people don't have to wake up alone if they don't want to." I answer, "But you make a promise, I mean I don't respect people who break marital promises." "Christ, you make a promise to get married when you're a twenty-three-year-old baby—do you think I'm the same person I was when I was twenty-three? I sat in library chairs and read biographies hoping I'd find some clue from other people's lives about how I was supposed to carry on mine. Unfortunately, it took me fifteen years to learn that reading biographies was one way not to lead my life. I'm a slow starter and a slow mover. It took me fifteen years to become a writer, and it took me ten years to get rid of that crazy woman I'd married because I thought I could help her."

"And me," I answer him, recognizing in my voice a forced self-definition, in imitation of him, "I follow people around as a journalist—watching them, analyzing their lives, looking for their secrets—because I'm afraid to face my own."

April 12

Yesterday at Schwartz's house the doorbell rang and a tall, gaunt man wearing a rumpled trench coat and a giant mustache marched into the living room. He had the face of a nightclub comedian who'd just heard his mother had died. I found myself peering out at him from the bedroom, uneasily making a few calls for an article for the *Times* I'm doing about the architect Louis Kahn, and wondering at the propriety of my presence. Finally I wandered out and met John Schwartz's friend, the writer Philip Roth. The two men have deliberately set out to acquire Jewish mannerisms much in the same way a drag queen learns to swish his hips and apply a cupid's bow to his mouth. After raising his eyebrows at me several times, a gesture John enjoyed but refused to acknowledge except by pregnant silence, Roth proceeded to question him about a recent trip to the Lenten carnival in Rio, a bacchanale that goes through several nights and days of music and drugs and orgy. "It was all sex," Schwartz shrugged, "boring to jaded sophisticates like us."

I was alternately appalled and admiring of his gall as John swung his hips and imitated one abundant and naked woman whose picture he waved in the air while he played the Festival samba music at earsplitting volume. He picked up some tambourine-like drums and started shaking them and pounding them as he swept around the room. Roth dolefully clapped his hands a few times to the music.

As soon as the music stopped, Roth went into his act. These two overanalyzed, over self-sensitized men have a campy ironic rapport. "John, Johnela," Roth whined, "your father and I, we've only wanted the best for you." He was wringing his hands and rocking gently back and forth, still hunched over in his trench coat. "Johnny, nobody could say we didn't try. The best colleges money could buy. Even a Ph.D., Johnny. Wait, I said. Don't get married. I'm an old woman, wait till I die. No, but you had to marry her, and then, so then? Divorced. And strange young women in your house in the afternoon, and crazy fershluggener dances. What will the neighbors think? John? John? So you don't even speak to your mother who loves you so?"

I was horrified. Suddenly I heard a laugh; my whole face had cracked and I was giggling and whooping, trying to catch my breath. Roth sighed, pulled himself to his feet, and casually picked up John's umbrella. "So my son, such a nice umbrella. One thing your father and I always said about you, some taste he has. He sure knows how to throw money around. Is it new?" He began stroking the umbrella gently with his palm. "So nice and long and thick and black, John. So masculine." And Roth curled his thumb and forefinger around the umbrella and began to slowly masturbate it. "Oh John. So masculine, I'm so proud of you." I was by this time blowing my nose and trying to get back under control, and the two men each threw me a shy glance. John was miffed, because Roth's act had gone over better. He pulled the umbrella away from Roth and snapped, "Yes, it is a new umbrella, I bought it in Rio."

Then I got a long appraising look from Philip Roth. I looked back while John was fussing with his samba records. "Take off your glasses," Roth said abruptly to me. I couldn't bring myself to make such an undignified gesture. So he leaned over and slowly took them off my face. "You have beautiful eyes, doesn't she look like that covergirl model we used to know, John?" John didn't look up. "No," he said testily. Roth threw me another dolorous look and lumbered to his feet. "Ladies and gentlemen, the afternoon's entertainment is over. Back to the typewriter. You know John, that doctor is doing wonderful things for my arm. Soon I'll be able to type again without agony. Good-bye." As John ushered him out in the hallway, I heard a few happy shouts and some whispers. I felt good. I'd just had the unexpected pleasure of watching a writer, who'd devoted a large part of his artistic life to motherhood and masturbation, act out both fantasies simultaneously.

Back in the apartment, John glared at me for a second. "Philip thinks you're pretty," he announced. "But you really did it. You embarrassed both of us by letting him pull your glasses off. I thought you women's libbers didn't want to be sex objects."

April 20

These afternoons fold in on each other like whipped cream in cocoa. I never quite know what is literary parody in his conversation, what is insanity, and what is unadorned truth. Anyway, I'm doing fieldwork on the American male. Nobody has ever confided in me with such intimacy and insight. We could talk forever. When I've had interesting experiences lately, the price is usually the article I must write. Now I am living for the experience alone.

John loves to shock me with his stories, like the one about his model girl friend who used to beg him to tie her up nude in a chair. Then she wanted him to order a large supply of groceries from Gristede's. Her fantasy was that when the delivery man would arrive through the open door,

John would be hiding and watching while the bewildered boy would yield to her cries and untie her. The punchline to these stories is always his own prudery. "How could I permit such a terrible thing? Me, a college professor. How could I ever allow such a thing under my roof?" And then his wild laugh.

He is a prurient Victorian who loves my reactions better than the stories themselves. He talks with feigned indifference about sex orgies with well-known literary married couples, of his ex-wife who, he claims, had a nervous breakdown the day they married and decided she had polio and couldn't have sex, and to whom he remained faithful for the ten joyless years they were married. He also tells me he is writing an autobiography of his graduate student days and we laugh about how he is asking all the different psychiatrists he's seen over the years for their tapes of his sessions. "Yeah," he giggles, "I called that last worthless sonofabitch and I hustled him for about ten minutes about how he could make a major contribution to literature if he'd dig up the notes and the tapes. 'Doc,' I said, 'it'll make us both immortal.' I'm so ashamed of myself. Anyway, he delivered. He called me back in that sepulchral Moses on the Mountain voice and read me a few choice dreams. There was one I'd had about leading the Philadelphia Orchestra in an academic gown around the time when I was thinking of leaving teaching for music criticism. So I moved my ass over to his doorman and picked up the tapes. God forbid we should meet face to face. But I got the tapes. I'll finally get my money's worth from him."

He also talks about his mother in a way that is not all caricature. She did in fact instruct him, "John, who needs to get married? Wait, wait a little John; when I'm dead, then you can run after women."

"We occasionally slept in the same bed until I was thirteen," he recalls. "And when I came home from college for Christmas I'd lie in the next room all night long and think, she's sleeping in there all by herself. I could just go in there and ram it right inside her—she's been asking for it, begging me for it all these years. Oh, she'd pretend to fight, but she's hot for me, I know it."

April 25

Lately, when I wake up in the middle of the night, I can't see Paul at all, but can make out only a huge pile of our feather comforter between us. I wonder if he is hiding from me. This morning he has disappeared from the bed and I hear him singing in the shower a Ray Charles song, "What'd I Say," that he hasn't sung for years. What's making him so cheery? I feel left out.

It's Saturday and I'm idly thinking about what hours I'm going to put in at the typewriter. I switch on the radio and I hear James Taylor singing "Fire and rain now . . ." the wind-up to his song. Then the disc jockey starts discussing Taylor's life and papers rustle and suddenly he's reading from the article I wrote about Taylor that has just appeared in the *Sunday Times Magazine*. I start calling for Paul to hear the radio. He emerges, wiping the water out of his hair with a giant orange towel draped around him. He looks like Tony Curtis playing the part of an Arabian sheik.

I remember the fuss he made when I bought the thick towels in bright orange and pink. He hates to spend money, and he hates me to spend money. But now he plays with the towels like they were new toys. I watch him wiping and wrapping his body in the bright fabric. But I don't understand how he can forget his pleasure each time I bring home a new purchase.

"Paul, listen, they're reading my article on WPLJ. It's great, isn't it?" Paul smiles. "Yeah, they're reading that part where you say what a great journalist you are." His words sting.

"But what are you talking about?" I say. "Listen to what he's reading," says Paul, burying his head in the towel. It's true that the guy on the radio is reading what I thought was the best part of the article—where I describe having stayed up till 3:00 A.M. with James while he slowly drank himself into a stupor and finally raised his arms like a Christ on the cross and said, "I like you, ask me anything you want." I wrote about the scene and also my reaction to him. I felt cheap, because as a journalist I had trailed this sensitive spacey kid, gotten him to trust me, and then I had taken his secrets and printed them.

I felt I had broken through my formalism by actually being able to write my feeling about that moment into the piece. "It's your hypocrisy," Paul is explaining as he takes the label off a new, tight striped knit shirt he bought yesterday on impulse. "On the one hand, you did milk the kid for all the private information you could get from him. On the other hand, you're saying how it broke your heart to do it." He's not looking at me as he talks, and I notice a slight sneer in profile—or maybe it's just my imagination.

"What're you up to?" I ask, changing the subject, hoping to change my mood. I am surprised to see him up so early on Saturday morning. The new shirt is a puzzle. He doesn't believe in buying himself things.

"Oh, didn't I tell you? Emily and I are walking over to the Navajo exhibit at the Metropolitan Museum and then we're going up to the Museum of the American Indian. There are some early Indian blankets she wants to show me. She says that they look like contemporary hard-edge paintings."

Another museum jaunt with Emily, the third in three weeks. Why can't I rate a Saturday with him? What's going on with Emily? I noticed she had been unduly interested in him at her party. Maybe I've been too self-absorbed lately.

As my temper rises, I sit up in bed. I am mad. I should tell Paul. But I am always embarrassing him with the excesses of my moods. Anyway, I can't face a confrontation this early in the morning. I have to think it over.

There's something about me that hates the morning. I'm a night person. I love to get a great conversation or a heavy emotional discussion going after twelve. It's also that I'm having a postpartum journalism letdown, I assure myself, because this Taylor article had worked out so well. I'd picked out a kid whose tunes went round and round in my head and I knew I had to listen to him in concert, and to write about someone who could write that music. Then the story had grown as he became a national figure. But it is finished now. And I have no projects to look forward to that could please me as this story has.

By now Paul is in the kitchen and I toss the covers off, pulling on my dungarees. I pad barefoot into the kitchen. I am wearing one of Paul's undershirts that I have taken to sleeping in. As he butters his toast, I watch him in silence. I sit with my chin in my hand and stare at him, wondering why he isn't looking at me. Maybe married people see each other so much they don't need to look at each other. What am I going to do with myself today, now that he's leaving?

Our doorbell chimes and he rushes to answer it. "No, nobody else here, just Susan and me," he is saying out in the hallway. I am puzzled by his remarks. "Oh, I see," Emily answers, looking at me over Paul's shoulder as they both enter the kitchen. Paul is uneasy with her, I muse. There's no reason to tell her nobody else is here except me. But he does have a habit of filling in silences with unimportant chatter.

"Hi," I say to Emily, noticing that she is wearing very heavy perfume. She's also wearing a lot of rouge and her red hair is washed and curled. She lights a cigarette as she sits down opposite me at the kitchen table. "Want some coffee?" I ask her, conscious that my unbrushed teeth, tangled hair, and torn man's undershirt are a sharp contrast to her perfume and curls. "Okay," she says, smiling at me. "Your James Taylor piece was just great," she says as I put a cup in front of her. "My children really think I'm somebody because I know the person who wrote it."

"Thanks," I say and start to talk rapidly about how it's hard to think of something to do next, because that piece was such fun. She's nodding her head. Paul interrupts me. He's been standing behind me. "We better get going, we have to beat the Saturday crowds at the museums. I'll be back at four, honey," he says, and pats my head.

I turn but he's already left the kitchen. I feel tired, Emily has just said nice things about my piece, but my mood hasn't improved. She picks up her purse and follows him out. She has left most of her coffee. I put her lipstick-stained cup into the sink, I empty the ashes of the two half-smoked cigarettes she's left behind during the five minutes she's been in our kitchen. A nervous, high-strung person, I note, washing her cup. Then I walk into the living room to stare at the telephone, wondering who I can call.

I devote five minutes to a long, silent stare at the phone, then I walk over to my desk and start to type. After about an hour, I go back into the kitchen to make myself a sandwich. As I open the mayonnaise my stomach turns over; Emily and Paul are having an affair. They could be touching each other right now. I remember her head on his thigh at her party. I can't think of him kissing another woman the way he kisses me.

April 27

Last night Emily called for some reason and I started talking to her. She began complaining about how she and her husband never really talk anymore. "After you've been married for a while you run out of things to talk about," I said, listening back for her answer. "Just like sex with someone you've been married to for six years just can't be as much fun as it is with a new person." I heard her inhale sharply. Then she asked me, "Do you want to go shopping with me Saturday?" In other words, I thought—feeling guilty that I wasn't more charmed—instead of having her Saturday date with Paul, she's going to look over the competition.

When I have such ambivalent thoughts I wonder first, am I crazy? How could anyone really be so sweet to me and be having a thing with Paul? Why do I insist her sharp intakes of breath, her museum dates and her party flirtation are predatory—am I a small-minded child in a world where adults live by rules I don't understand?

After I agreed to our Saturday shopping excursion, Paul, who had been standing in the doorway of the living room during part of our conversation, picked up the extension in the kitchen. "Hiya, Emily," he said. "Oh, hi, I gotta get off," she stammered.

Our excursion was strange. Paul, who hates shopping, had agreed earlier to drive us to a new boutique and then take her VW station wagon back to our house. He pounded the horn, drove through two red lights, and twisted the steering wheel to avoid the hordes of upper West Side pedestrians. Emily sat between us, her eyes on the sidewalk screamers and stalled traffic.

Inside, the store was decorated in Art Deco curvy-clean designs of white and silver, and the rooms hummed with the sound of a French female singer who ends her song in orgasmic pants unadulterated by music. I discovered a long dress, plain enough except for silver threads running through the gray. Emily's arms were soon filled with brightly colored T-shirts, blues and greens. The dressing room, with its red velvet walls and mirrors everywhere, looked like a disorganized bordello. While the French singer moaned, the young women in the dimly lit room pulled shirts over their heads, revealing breasts and trim torsos. A tall woman next to me slipped off her buckskin bellbottoms to stand nude except for her tiny black lace bikini. She pulled a black evening gown over her head and wriggled until it clung to her body.

Emily put down her pocketbook, slipped off her beige car coat and pulled her orange short sweater over her tousled hair. She stood there in her bra, her stomach bare. I watched her, wondering if Paul had touched her breasts. Impossible. I felt less tense. Still, my eyes measured their proportions. She looks better in clothes. As an artist, she knows how best to dress. Small breasts, no waistline, and slim legs, she wears tight polo shirts and short skirts. But my mind kept returning to the idea of her body in the act of making love. I was watching her watch herself in the huge round mirror. I stared at her tiny trim breasts and white stomach hanging out slightly above her miniskirt. She kept tugging on the shirts and turning her body to observe herself. I was pleased that the shirts were too tight. My small victory.

By then I had slipped off my workshirt and was pulling on the silver lamé dress. I always wear dungarees, but when I go shopping I often try on evening gowns. What does this mean about my fantasies? The gown looked okay; since I have started seeing John Schwartz and worrying about Paul, I have lost five pounds. My stomach is practically concave. My face looks tired, and there are new lines between the outside of my nose and the outside of my mouth.

"You look fantastic," Emily watched me with a big grin, still clutching her shirts in her arms. I warmed up toward her. Maybe she's just a lonely lady who wants to make friends.

"You're so lucky," she continued in a rush. "I mean my husband would never drive me shopping. You have the best of everything—the most interesting career of anyone I know and a fantastic husband."

I don't want her evaluating me or my husband. The small excess of her words hung between us until she groped nervously in her handbag for a cigarette. Standing in her bra and skirt, she steadied one elbow against her other palm as she inhaled one puff after another. Her fingers were shaking. "Well," she was still talking, since I said nothing but was pulling on my dungarees, "make up your mind, Sue, and let's get going. I'd say buy it, but you look swell in anything you put on."

We walked out into the street in silence. Neither of us had bought anything. Back at my house she suggested I go up and tell Paul to bring down her car keys. "See you next week," she called after me. "What?" I half-turned and shaded my eyes against the sun shining over Central Park behind her. "Paul accepted for you. You're coming to my house for a small dinner party. You'll like the group, you'll see."

MAY

May 1

Some days my life feels badly edited. I find myself in happy scenes like John Schwartz's afternoons and then in miserable traps with new characters and new backdrops.

It's hard to remember the silly fun of meeting Philip Roth when I feel that something is making Paul manic and it's not me. He's dancing more often at night in front of the mirror to Tammy Wynette singing "Stand By Your Man" with earphones on so I can't even hear the musical stimulation. And last night he had a highly emotional discussion with Alice about how, although you love some people, you can't spend your life with them. At the James Taylor concert I had invited him to tonight, he sang the songs out loud and swayed his body and shook his head with his eyes closed. I forced myself to ignore him as I watched the kids around us give him angry looks. Later in the grocery store, when I picked out an expensive frozen quiche Lorraine, he slammed a bag of apples, bread, and milk on the floor of the store with disgust. "Can't you be trusted in a store at all?" he screamed, and stomped out, walking down Broadway in the opposite direction from our house. I felt like another sordid

New York scene that everybody was looking away from as I pushed a few apples back into his shopping bag. Then he was leaning down helping me gather the slightly torn bag's contents together. "I'm sorry, honey," he said sadly. "This evening has not gone well. I thought it'd be fun to have a date together. But it didn't work out." We walked home in silence. I felt unwilling to face the fact that I was screaming silently for help.

May 5

This afternoon I exploded. I enjoyed the eruption after being careful not to reveal my tensions to Paul recently.

"I am not going to any more of those boring parties," I shouted. "How dare you accept another invitation for me when you know I don't like them? I find those people a total waste of time."

My voice sounded harsh and self-pitying. "I don't have any compulsion to go there. The only reason for these parties is that someone is enjoying the public face of a private flirtation. You can go there and flirt with Emily if you want, but why drag me to watch?" There it was, out, the ugly, self-terrorizing fantasy made into sounds, words. Part of me truly believed that if I never said the words, the ideas would disappear just as my childhood fear of the dark, then of school, then of millions of other pieces of my life had disappeared after the initial panic.

And in recent years, it had been Paul who had assumed the responsibility for brushing away these terrors, correcting my perceptions of reality. "Go back there and *ask* him how he put together that skit, don't let some public relations man scare you away," he ordered me out of the house when I was reporting for an article on an educational television show and was banned from the studio. "Oh, just write any lead, any beginning like this . . ." he'd say as I'd wring my hands, knowing I'd never find the perfect way to start an article. He'd sit down fearlessly at my typewriter and type out a paragraph. "No, no," I'd explain, and galvanized by his energy, but sure his beginning wasn't right, I'd sit down to write. And emotionally, Paul had been the interpreter too. "Just because Ann didn't return your call doesn't mean she doesn't want to be your friend," he'd say soothingly in New Haven. Or when I felt really out of it at faculty parties where I believed everybody was doing more interesting work than I was, he'd make a point of telling me, "Al's wife thinks you're a dynamo—working at your telephone company job and taking those writing classes, too."

Now he would come through once more and erase my fears of the past two weeks. "Don't worry so much," he said harshly, running his hands through his hair. I put my arms on his shoulders from behind and said pleadingly, "Paul, do me a favor and don't tell anyone about this conversation—including Emily." "Okay, okay, of course," he promised, walking out of my hug. His words were only slightly soothing. Since I have started lying to him, I can't really trust anything he says to me.

May 10

For the last few days the apartment has been filled with people. On spring vacation, old friends from Yale feel it their right to stay with us. Mornings my temper flares as I confront Barry's new handlebar mustache and Maoist ideology over his wheat germ. Not only is he intruding here where tension is high, but he has a graduate student's condescension toward my bourgeois life-style. I have taken to nasty barbs about Emily disguised as humor. I am too proud to plead for Paul's reassurance.

Yesterday I asked, "Does she dye her hair red? I guess her pubic hair is gray. Isn't it, dear?" His head leaps a little, as I jab at him this way. I wish I could stop, but I feel a false sense of power because I can still make nasty jokes to capture his attention. You're the bitch, I tell myself after one of these assaults on him. You're the bitch all right as Paul answers sadly, "Poor Emily, you shouldn't say things like that Susan, it's cruel." It is pride—no, arrogance—that makes me seek reassurance by punching at him. "No, no," he should say, "You are the only woman whose pubic hair I have seen in the last ten years."

But why should he, on the other hand, even understand what it is I am asking for with my snide little attacks? Do I understand? As I turn a plate under the kitchen faucet or push a cart through the supermarket, whole scenes keep repeating in my head. "I hate you. I want you to leave this house," I tell him, drawing a sharp breath with the impact of these words even in fantasy, "I can manage without you. If you get so much pleasure out of Emily, be with her. I don't need you."

Here I pause. In my fantasy, he has two alternatives. "No," he says, beginning his good response, "I'll never leave you." My answer is then angry. "Well, who needs you? I love you Paul, but you're so fucking distant right now. This is not the perfect life we promised each other." But he's stalwartly sweet. "One more chance, Susan. We're both changing. Just because I choose different friends from yours or different ways of having fun—like reading books and going to museums—doesn't mean that we weren't meant to spend our lives loving each other."

But Paul is not so reassuring lately. And in my fantasy, the other way he could respond to my anger is with his own anger. "Okay, so fuck you. I have more fun when I'm not

with you. I don't love you." While I am picturing this conversation I start to cry, but then I stop as my anger reasserts
itself. "Oh yeah, I can live okay on my own too, you know.
Remember all those times I was reporting on stories. I could've
gotten to spend more time away. I could go out with John
Schwartz at night to movies." Then my stomach turns over
as I try to think of what it would be like to lose Paul as the
central person in my life. Then, of course, there's the obvious
reason why I've no right to be angry at all. First I slept with
Jim St. Clare, then John Schwartz. And John Schwartz talks
my language and forces me to talk back to him in new ways.
But I get no comfort thinking about him. Instead I feel
trapped by my actions that come from motivations I don't
understand.

Yesterday, I sat with John for a half hour in the late
afternoon in his living room, and he said, after a long silence,
"So honey-pot, gumdrop, so where's your husband in all of
this? You're not still in love with him, are you? I mean, how
could you be—and still be here with me?" I answered him
before I'd thought the words. It feels painful because I am
defining by myself—without Paul. "I love Paul and I believe
we love each other—but right now we are distant from each
other. It's just temporary growing pains that any long-term
relationship has to go through."

He laughed a short snort. "I mean okay, not every night
and every afternoon—that's square—but how many hours a
week do you spend together in loving companionship? How
many times a week do you fuck, anyway? No," he held his
hand up as I stumbled into an answer, "spare me, please.
I don't want to hear some idealized bullshit picture of your
sex life. It'd hurt me too much. And if I forced you to say it,
you might start believing it."

Lately I am sexually aggressive with Paul. Maybe it's
the same energy that made me taunt him about Emily. Or
maybe since I am having new sex with John, I am simply

more sexual. Tonight I came home and found Paul sleeping on the couch in the living room, a book lying on its front on top of his stomach. When I walked over to him he opened an eye and his arm in a welcoming hug. I scrunched onto the couch next to him.

After I've seen John, I see Paul as vulnerable, a person wronged. As we started to stroke and hug each other, he smiled a big sleepy smile. But when I started to move to kiss his body, he stopped me with a vague gesture. "No, honey. Don't do that." Immediately I was wary. Why not? Was I being protected from the smell or taste of another woman. I clenched my teeth silently as he bent to kiss my mouth.

May 15

Two afternoons ago, John sat close to me on his black suede sofa and worried out loud about his finances. Then he announced that he was going to get Jackie Kennedy's interior decorator to redo his living room. He sounded silly. His preoccupation with style seems dumb.

Then he switched once again to his antimarriage rap. "So, you come here three days a week, sugarpie, and so you're still a married lady. What's the score? I mean, what do you get out of that marriage? Tell me, I'm really interested in the way your sweet little mind works. Your sweet little kinky mind —I mean it's kinky, isn't it, you coming here afternoons and going home to your loving husband at night, or is he loving, puss? Tell, tell. Why be married?"

"I don't like to sleep alone," I said hurriedly, trying to sound as practical as he does. "Oh, don't be naive. I tell you yet you refuse to hear. You're an attractive woman, and you don't have to sleep alone for ten seconds ever if you don't feel like it."

"I have shared a past with Paul," I said, hating the mawkish sound to my words, but determined to rise to the confrontation, "and I don't want to lose it." He laughed. We locked eyes for a moment. I felt angry. "Aah, I made her mad, well lookit, doll, how do you lose your past if you and your husband split up? You're still you, with twenty-nine years of living experience under your belt and you still have lived through five years of marriage with him."

"Well, I made a pact and it's part of my past and I don't want to go back on my word. It has to do with integrity," I said, with a wave in the air, knowing that I'd pushed the conversation into the realm of the sentimental where he could make me sound like a fool.

"Dear heart, you made that transcendent marital vow of all vows when you were how old?" "Twenty-three." "Were you still on the bottle? You were a different person then. You had no career, no self-confidence. You're a long way from having self-confidence as your everyday companion, but you've changed. And you wouldn't be here if that guy was giving you everything you wanted, sugarlump."

"Well, I love him," I said, pushed to the wall.

"I'm not going to quibble with that, dear. But you and your husband sound pretty distant to me. Love can't be just a fantasy. Something current has to be going on, baby." I remembered Paul piling the comforter cover between us in bed, hiding from me.

John gets the last word. Sophistication, cynicism, and selfishness, I tell myself. Nonetheless every time I reveal some terror about life after marriage, he explodes my fears, and I feel better for a while. Maybe I would survive and even prosper without a husband. Just the idea gives me a tightening of my shoulders. I wondered bleakly as I entered our apartment if I should start taking tranquilizers, and tried to remember how Paul's wife, who just spent an extra-long day at the office, would look and act as she came home and greeted her husband.

Paul has disappeared for the day—a Saturday—to work on his book at the office. I followed him belligerently to the door, noting the briefcase and the special jacket he wears to school. Of course he's going to school, I told myself.

I'll work, too. It takes me as long to make myself sit down to work as I actually spend working. If I could get over this fear of starting, I would spend twice as much time writing. John and I talk compulsively about writing. We've discussed the problems of topic sentences for paragraphs, book chapters without climaxes, and metaphors so pretentious they make a paragraph look shabby. He also claims that writers drink a little to help themselves begin. At first I thought he was weird, sipping his Scotch as he wrote each day. But he'd explain how it made him less afraid of his typewriter, as though he could confide to it.

Yesterday I found some brandy under our kitchen cabinet and poured a one-quarter-inch into an orange juice glass. At my desk I sipped it, ruminating about how I was going to start writing. Suddenly I knew exactly what had to be done. It wasn't until I finished the second page that I realized the brandy had worked.

May 19

Yesterday Paul returned from a one-day ski trip with swollen knees. He's decided to go skiing for the first time with some N.Y.U. colleagues even though I chose not to go. I reproached him for overexerting. When I realized that I was nagging, I walked to the drugstore to buy some Heet—which I smeared on his knees to make a grandmotherly dankish smell in the bed where he was lying in a trance. Paul keeps surprising me in ways that make me uneasy. I don't tolerate the same romanticism in him that I would enjoy in a man I was less involved with. If Paul were to assess women's physical assets as lewdly as John does, I'd go bananas. But the "husband" must behave with a certain asexual restraint. I wonder if this bugs Paul. "Paul," I asked him, flopping myself next to the warm bundle he made under the covers, "what are you thinking about?" "I'm thinking about being at college," he answered me, staring dreamy-eyed at the ceiling. "What about college?" "I'm thinking how much fun it was to be bad and irresponsible and be a kid and all."

He has kept a discreet silence when I've asked him if he finds a woman attractive. Undoubtedly he senses my panic at the thought of him with another woman—why do I write undoubtedly? I don't know.

But yesterday I persisted. "Like what irresponsible things did you do?" I felt the impending pain. "Oh," and his voice was trembling slightly, "I guess I mean fights and adventures —like the time the sophomore threatened to beat me up because I had spent the night with his steady girl friend, and I had to hide in another girl's bedroom."

"Had you slept with the guy's girl friend?" I asked again, dreading his answer and wondering why the hell I was making the inquisition. "What? Oh yeah, of course." Paul smiled. "What'd you think?"

"Honey," I pouted, pretending a childish pique, "how come you never told me till now? I always thought you were pure when I captured you." Of course, I knew he wasn't.

"Are you kidding?" he answered, ignoring my question about why now, "I went out with at least six women before you. What did you think I was anyway?"

Why is he opening up like this? Why is he thinking about his adolescent sex life? What has changed for him? I dare not think about it now. I must distract myself.

Last night I dreamed that someone had cut my throat by accident and I was convalescing while it healed. Paul's sex life. If he loved me even though he slept with other women, why am I suddenly so threatened by the knowledge? He married me, didn't he? But why?

Paul says he's going to the office again, so I decide to take a bike ride over to the East Side and John's house.

As I bike through the park, I see a brownish gray rat on the path behind the Metropolitan Museum. On Fifth Avenue I watch the parade of people. When I first came here I thought New Yorkers looked overcolored, overpainted. Today when I go back to campuses, I feel I have to strain my eyes to see the kids who seem out of focus with unpainted lips and cheeks, wearing dowdy beige or khaki green shapeless sweaters, crumpled workshirts and dungarees.

As I bike over to his street, I smile at the shorter hairstyles the women are wearing. Sometimes I worry about my new-found New York interest, my fascination with surfaces. Today I see a woman with soft pink-beige high boots on. I wheel my bicycle around passersby as I follow her and her small brown dog down Fifth Avenue. She hails a cab, and I realize I have to make my move. "I really like your boots," I say. "Where'd you get them?" "Bergdorf's." I am happy; the rat is forgotten, the boots will be very chic. But how long will they last? And what about my serviceable brown leather boots that I wore through rain and snow in New Haven? The seashell-pink suede won't make it through one slushy snow, and I don't want to become a style fiend, too.

In New Haven, I was safe. I was outside the Yale community. I could not become an academic snob and there was no other kind of snob to be. I could only feel an uneasy desire to poke away at the pretensions and elitist poses of the academics—genteely laughing at the rest of the world living in the here and now while they were studying the great works of the past, or imparting knowledge of them to the kids, to the people who owned the future. In New York, people get points for being wickedly extroverted, flashy, amusing in conversation, and aware of trends, and I am no longer the disapproving outsider.

In New York, I have found an identity. The first week I was here, I published an article in the brand new *New York* magazine. In their office, at parties, or interviewing people for articles, I suddenly found the best work identity I'd ever had in my life. I took solemn pride in telling people who asked me at parties what I did, "I am a free-lance journalist." "And what's *that* supposed to mean?" asked the wife of the chairman of the N.Y.U. History Department as she danced past me on the arm of a young assistant professor. Instead of going into a wrongway tail slide, I smiled back at her, confident that the mistake was hers. "I write for *New York* magazine and the *Times Magazine* on a nonsalaried basis," I said smiling. Two years before a semisarcastic question, "And what do you *do* at the Telephone Company?" would have upset me for two days.

Despite its flaws, New York is the only place I want to be. If the academic world looked dull to me as an outsider, in New York I will struggle to be serious, to find the seriousness here.

I passed the afternoon looking at John's family photograph album, which quickly became pictures of his former girl friends—a staged studio portrait of a former model and a page of a detective magazine showing a girl in a bikini tied to a chair; she turns out to be a former amour who is currently trying to make it in publishing. I sat passively entertained as he rolled out his anecdotes about his past and his views of life. None of it threatens me—neither his selfishness nor what I begin to understand is his sexual finickiness—he rejects most women on the basis of flaws in their beauty, or so he claims. I tell myself that I don't care what his sexual tastes are, how loyal or disloyal he is to his friends—measurements that I take once every three minutes on Paul. Because John is an adventure, I do not worry about whether or not I trust him. I am happy about this state. I know where my emotional commitment is. Today, I feel like I'm doing an article about him.

At our house, Paul sat with his back to me as I entered the dining room. I walked behind him, repeating my greeting. "Well," I said, "hello, dear." And I repeat, "Hello, dear," and Paul turned around with a shamefaced smile as though I'd surprised him doing something illegal. "I made dinner," he explained. "Oh, how wonderful." During the past two weeks of his diet he has been looking gaunt, with hollows in his cheeks and a trimmer line to his stomach and buttocks. He's gotten vainer and bought himself a pair of tight pants. But I didn't like the short cuff and the tight legs. When I turned up his pants cuff to see if the hem could be let down and muttered that he should spend more than six dollars for pants in the future, he walked away from my appraising hands.

Tonight he'd made a special Adelle Davis low-calorie cabbage soup. As we sat down at the table, he dramatically ladled the clear red soup into huge bowls. We slurp in silence until the back doorbell rings. Alice had come up to chat. Paul offered her soup. She blew on a spoonful, laughed, and whispered to me, "Paul the maid. He's a jewel. I'd hire him to come and cook and clean my house anytime. He could even sleep over."

Paul's eyes met mine with some coldness. I rushed into the conversation: "He isn't a maid, Alice." But as she giggled, I smiled involuntarily. "I do some work around the house too, you know. Paul just likes to help out, that's all."

He nodded. "Yeah, today our neighbor Carol called me into her kitchen and plied me with questions for about an hour about why I am such a good husband. She didn't say maid, but husband." "Did you know she's leaving Herb?" asked Alice, eating the last bits of translucent cabbage with eager fingers. "Yeah, she told me," Paul continued. "And what she was really trying to figure out was why I have so much respect for Susan and her work and I want to help around the house and everything and Herb, her husband, couldn't care less." "Wonderful, dear." I muttered with a fake sigh. "When are they going to plaster your picture up on every streetlight as the world's most perfect husband? It's a shame the woman doesn't get a lot of points from having picked out the world's most perfect man to marry, or I'd have made it too."

"Paul," I went on helplessly, "it occurs to me that you're the world's most perfect young assistant professor—tenure last year at the age of twenty-nine. You're also the world's most perfect husband. You're the most perfect everything. How do you do it?" As I spoke, I felt hysteria around my eyes. Maybe I am tired of being married to the world's most perfect person.

"C'mon, Susan," Alice heard my tension, "you are doing okay. You're doing journalism. Gosh, you're a real writer."

"Wait a minute, I want to show you some real writing." Paul jumped up from the table, knocking his new slimmer hip against a corner of the table in an effort to get out fast. He returned holding typewritten pages reverently with both palms. "I wrote the most amazing short story today. I really think it's very publishable. I'm not sure what it means."

As Alice nodded with enthusiasm, her eyes riveted on the first page, I wondered why he hadn't told me he'd written a story. In fact why—and I felt the familiar anger mixed up with hurt—why did he drag out the short story in the middle of Alice's compliment to me about my writing? I wished I wasn't seeing this as a competition, but I was. Paul has to be the star, the best at everything, in the same way that he's been the best at spousely duties. I never asked the perfect husband and the brilliant thinker to credit his feeble wife. Now he won't even let me be the writer in the family.

Alice flipped through his pages, and I marveled at his self-confidence. I can't show my writing to anyone except him until days after I've rewritten and reread it. If I tell Paul how angry I am, I'll sound like a selfish kid. But I felt as if he had just hit me with the full force of his flexible and huge ego. Just as I finally picked an area to work in, he confidently walked into the central square and started erecting his work of art.

I pushed my chair wearily from the kitchen table. "What's the matter, dear?" he asked, reading his manuscript upside down across the table.

"Ah, I'm really tired. I think I'm coming down with something. I'm going to sleep." Feeling bent nearly double with fatigue, I dragged myself to bed. I dreamed I was Paul dancing up a mountain waving a giant manuscript. I was also Susan in terrible pain, left behind sitting on an old beach chair and squinting into the horizon to find Paul. As I sat there wishing I could dance, too, I stood up. But then I quickly sat down, overwhelmed by rejection.

Suddenly I heard him, through my deep, sleepy breaths, whispering to me, "Honey, I'm going back to the office. I have to do some last-minute research for tomorrow's lecture. See you later."

I opened an eye to watch him striding quickly out of the bedroom, his briefcase swinging at his side. Then an hour later I woke myself up and switched on the light to stare at the chandelier on my ceiling. Some of my most intense feelings come when I am waking up alone, climbing to the surface of my psyche.

I swung my legs over the side of the bed and walked slowly toward the kitchen, turning on lights as I went. As I opened the cabinet door, looking for fruit juice, I heard the front door key and the door opening. I pulled out a box of cocoa and Paul walked into the kitchen, his briefcase in his hand. The phone rang, and he answered it, hung up. "It's Alice. She wants to come up again. Her husband's gone out for the evening."

He left the kitchen and as his bathroom door slammed, she rang the back bell.

"So."

"So?" We don't have to waste a lot of words talking. We've been best friends since we were eighteen and before that we knew each other a bit in high school. Paul and I moved into this apartment directly above hers in spite of his mild protests, but I haven't regretted it. She and I have few secrets. Just yesterday I told her about my thing with John Schwartz. One morning I thought we really parodied each other when she did a kind of swimming breaststroke on her side on the kitchen floor, in an effort to describe a great new sexual position she and her husband had discovered.

Tonight she peered at me. "What's with you?"

"I'm fidgety. Paul keeps going off on these work binges at the office. I'm not sure I believe there's anything inside his briefcase." "Why not look?" she giggled at me, daring me to do the act while assuring me by her light tone that she thought I was crazy. The phone rang, and Paul yelled, "I got it, it's Michael."

"Okay, now or never." I rushed out into the living room, checking the familiar clutter for the briefcase. I found it buried under Paul's coat and carried it into the kitchen. I threw it onto the kitchen table and unsnapped the front two buttons. "Voilà, the cupboard is bare," I started to say before examining its contents. But my voice sagged. There were two empty envelopes in the briefcase. Of course he could have left his work at the office, but still, I hissed at Alice, "He's probably humping that overage redhead in his office."

"Susan, you're too much. Poor Paul. He's not doing anything wrong. Anyway, you're having an affair. Why can't he?" Of course this is the great unanswerable question. How come only Susan can have a new romance in her life? Isn't Paul a person—so why shouldn't I wish him the best and happiest experiences? Because—as my shrink keeps telling me in her most disparaging voice—I tend to think of people as possessions, and Paul most of all is irrationally mine. I believe his actions reflect on me. I don't want him to be sharing his genitals with another woman.

Then he returned, his eye hit his open briefcase, and Alice and I exchanged glances. "What's going on?" he asked, closing the case and lifting it in one authoritative motion off the kitchen table. "It's me, the jealous nag. I wondered why if you were so hard at work your briefcase was empty," I dared explain in the hope that the moment was lightened because Alice was present. "Susan," he said, "I'm going out for a walk with Michael when he comes by. Why don't you and Alice finish that cabbage soup?"

"What about the question, dear? What were you doing at the office today, feeling up Emily, or vice versa?" I keep wondering why I persist in sour humor—again it's my act called "I'm so tough I'm not going to beg or even show how limp and miserable the idea of him loving someone else makes me." I'm going to act like a killer. "Poor Emily," Paul interrupted my ranting. "She likes you, Susan. You shouldn't be so mean." "She likes me plenty," I choked at Alice as he disappeared. "She likes me and wants to be my friend, Paul keeps telling me. And I hate her and make mean jokes. Well, aren't I the sweetheart?" I was sputtering as my anger turned to self-disgust. Alice sighed, "I still don't think you have much of a leg to stand on, and anyway she's not that much competition. Just take it easy."

By midnight, Paul and Michael returned to the apartment where I was dispiritedly watching television in the bedroom. "Hi, honey." Paul kissed the top of my head and left the room as fast as he'd come in. "Wait," I called, "when are you coming to sleep?"

Since silence was my answer, I heaved myself to my feet and walked barefoot into the living room. Michael sat on the edge of the couch and didn't look up at me. "Hiya," I waved briefly at him, and flopped into a chair. "What's with you, Michael? You look glum." "Oh, do I?" Michael tittered to prove he wasn't glum.

Maybe Paul told him, my voice shouted inside my head. He told him he loved Emily. No, he told him he's having an affair with Emily. He just told him he's worried because I'm having an affair with John. Maybe I'm hallucinating.

"Paul, I'm going in to sleep. What about you?" He looked at Michael. "I'm not tired now, and Michael's got some good grass, so go without me." I was humiliated by his rejection and realized how I must have irritated Paul for years with my inability to go to bed on time. Many nights he'd come out into the living room wearing his pajamas where I'd be talking with Alice or Carol, he'd stretch and yawn and say, "Now, come to bed now." I'd wait a few minutes, then say a nervous good-night, and join him. But tonight with our positions reversed, I lacked his authority.

May 22

I sat on the edge of our rumpled bed and stared at my feet, absently flexing and reflexing my toes. If I could only control my temper things would be all right. But what things? Marriage is not kept together for the sake of appearances but for emotional sustenance, and my mind raced along—what emotional sustenance am I getting from him when he goes off for walks with Michael, museum trips with Emily, and throws tantrums when I won't go to parties with him? Maybe that's the wife's role—to pretend all's right with your private world, and you put on a public face and go to parties. Last night, I tried a question about our private world before we fell asleep. "Paul, do you believe a person can love another person forever?" His answer scared me so I stopped the questions.

"Yes," he said, "but you also can love a new person, too, and yet not want to change your life or set up housekeeping with them."

Paul came into the bedroom, his eyes flashing, but avoiding mine. "Look, I feel like staying up," he said, flicking the television on and off. I was flooded with anger as though someone had shot a quart of it undiluted into my bloodstream. First came the comforter piled between us, and now he couldn't bear to get in bed next to me at night. God damn him. As this flashed through my mind, I also knew that I couldn't rely on this fury, that it would crumble into self-pity.

"What's the matter," I said, jumping to my feet, "you want to go back to the *office* and do some more work? And did you fuck on the desk, or maybe in the hallway right outside your office? Is it better than renting a motel?"

"And what the hell are you talking about?" he screamed back at me, and with a start I realized that I would not have to mine much further to find Paul's anger toward me.

"I'm talking about the fact that you have been ignoring me and telling secrets to Michael and carrying around an empty briefcase and saying you're working all the time and smiling to yourself."

"Okay," he shouted at me, his voice trembling, and while I recognized he was the new enemy, I still had to restrain the impulse to hug him, to pat him. But I didn't hug him, I stood there and waited for the nightmare to begin. I was hoping I was wrong, but I knew Paul had abandoned our coupleness. In a funny way it feels like his decision. He's in charge of us. It's all part of our agreement that he's the objective, clear-headed one. We've always acted as though my fears, my temper must be ignored or balanced by his saner, more adult view of life.

A married couple is like a car that has two steering wheels and two motors—sometimes the car jerks from side to side of the road, sometimes it moves ahead faster than all cars with just one steering wheel. My parents shared the belief that cigarettes were vile, that perfume gave them stomachaches, that vitamin pills were to be gulped in great number, that at times you can belch loudly in living rooms. I don't like these things, but felt I was a lunatic as I was growing up because the couple that was my parents believed them in such unison.

In the past months, Paul and I have been tearing away at the myths that made us a couple. I had decided that John was better company right now than Paul. Paul had decided he was tired of depriving himself for years of things I disapproved of, like museum visits, nude swimming, and dancing in front of the mirror wearing a stereo headset. We have stopped lurching from side to side and come to a dead stop. The moment had arrived. He'd yelled, "Okay." And I was watching and listening, my whole body tense.

Then, of course, there should have been a lot of movie organ music. I should have gotten a gold star for guessing correctly. But nothing happened except he smiled and looked happy and strong from having made a new liaison that left me out—and said, "Yes I am sleeping with Emily." Because I'd been trying to force out of him with every nasty crack I could think of, I felt the muscles in my upper shoulders and legs release—at last it's out in the open. Then I began to blame myself for having forced him to tell me.

So I who have difficulty crying, especially in front of other people, suddenly began to weep. Great spasms of tension in my chest and throat kept the tears coming. It was perhaps the most immediate reaction I've ever had to my own pain. Sometimes I have to sit back and think, so am I in pain now or not? Thus part of me was proud that I would do such a dramatically correct thing as cry at this point.

As I sob, I savor my hatred for Emily—her spoken adulation of him and of me has kept me from admitting it. But I can never bear to be in her presence again. She has already heard a whole new series of complaints about me that I will hear tonight mostly for the first time. And among the foul thoughts that I will have during the next few hours will be the idea that he needed her help to indict me and our relationship so completely. I hate her. And I hate her because he is using her to escape me—and escape his more innocent childish self to become as adult and cynical as John Schwartz. For a second I understand that Paul and I must shed each other, our first loves. But this explanation only modulates the pain for the briefest second.

And then it starts. One more question from me, a sour, morose me who knows that tonight is altering my life's history. Paul is in a private pleasure dome. His eyes are glittery with excitement and he reaches out to grab me and say, "Susan, I like you very much, I didn't want to hurt you."

I don't believe him and feel the answering rage as though he'd just said, "I have been hurt and angry with you and now I want to hurt you back." He's standing above me as I sit in a huddle. One question: "Do you love her, Paul?" He looks as though he's a puppet being twitched around in a show of happiness by invisible strings. "Yes, I love her."

"What about me, Paul? What about me?" I stand in a half-crouch and point both forefingers at my chest—a reproaching hag, I think abruptly and sit down, collapsed in impotence. He answers, "You, dear? I like you very much. But I don't think I love you."

Where to start? How cunning shall I be? Shall I be gentle and try to bring him back? I transmute my anger into guile and pleasantry. "Paul, dear," I say to my surprise rather sweetly, putting my hand on his arm. And at that he wrenches away, his brow darkening. I perceive he will be happy now only if I am miserable. As I struggle for control, his anger shows. How he must hate me. No, that's not it, it's just that we're so carefully balanced a team that if he shows happiness I must show pain, or if I show self-control he can afford a fit, a temper tantrum. No, that's not it, he hates me. He hates me as only an intimate can hate you, a person who watches you clean your ears with Q-Tips, moan over menstrual cramps, lie to public relations men over the telephone, or cry at the rejection of an article. He hates me because he is the only person whom I've allowed to see me.

"Of course you love me, Paul. I mean you've loved me in the past, haven't you?"

"No, we shouldn't have gotten married when we did. I was too young and lonely from being in graduate school. I've always liked you very much but I never loved you."

"You liar," I bellow at him, raising my fist. "You goddam fucking liar. You can't rewrite my life. I love you. Don't you think I need you, Paul?"

"Emily needs me more than you do," he says stoutly, his brow uncreasing as soon as I lose my newfound self-control and find my temper. "And I've spent my last night masturbating," he continues. "Yes, masturbating because you were depressed or preoccupied and didn't feel like screwing." Shocked, I keep watching his face. I feel nauseated; he looks like someone I've never met. Then I start to cry as he becomes an achingly familiar and somewhere lovable person whom I've failed.

"Don't you think I love you, Paul?" I persist in the supposition that he's been hurt by me. I want to reassure him. "Emily loves more sides of me than you do," he recites, sounding to me like a robot who's just learned a new series of key phrases.

"But how can she love more of you? I have known you for ten years and I know more of you and love you on the basis of all that time. You've known her for a few months."

"She loves more of me. She doesn't criticize me the way you do."

"Paul," I beg him, "when I criticize you, it's like criticizing myself. Of course I take too many mood changes out on you. But please don't ever say I don't love you. I've loved you since I was nineteen years old."

"That's the trouble," he interrupts, "you love a past me. And it's a past you with childish needs who loves a past vision of me."

Several times I leave the room to pace the dark apartment. "Yes," he whispers when I ask him, as though the subject is sacred, "Emily and I do have better sex than you and I have." I feel as if he has kicked me. As I pace the hallway, I am a general planning the next battle: he's still talking about me and him in the present, even though he says he loves her. Then my stomach turns with fear, and several times I retreat to the bathroom. I think: I'm still alive, my body still works. Then I shake my head in disbelief as I think they've slept together. When? I shuffle back into the bedroom. Paul has put on his blue flannel pajamas. He smiles vaguely at me, as he turns down the sheet. "When"—I practically pant—"when did she seduce you?" He pats my head with pity. "She didn't seduce me. The whole thing was my idea. Emily really likes you and didn't want to start anything with me, but I forced it. She's a very vulnerable person." I rush with fresh tears out of the bedroom. I'm not sleeping in that bed next to him. At the living room closet I wave futilely in the air for the light chain, and then grope in the dark till I feel my coat. I'm getting out of here, now, I whisper aloud. I don't have to take this humiliation.

Instead of leaving, I stumble back in the bedroom half into my coat. "I'm going for a walk." I am snuffling, teary. "Oh, honey, don't go out there by yourself, it's 3:00 A.M. I'll get dressed and go with you, if you want." He dutifully switches on the light and squints at me.

"No, I don't need you to go for a walk at night. First you knock me down and then you pretend you're my nursemaid. Let me alone." I squeeze my arm past the hole in my sleeve lining and march to the front door. He walks quickly after me and stands blocking the door, his hand on the door-knob behind him. "No, don't go yourself. It isn't safe. Come to sleep." He absently kisses the top of my head in the old way and I feel hope. The new feeling—infatuation, whatever he has for Emily—has not destroyed the rituals of our love for each other: his head-top kiss, his use of the word honey, his desire to protect me and keep me from wandering around at night. It's like I told John Schwartz. We're just very distant from each other. In the dark, at our living room door, I believe if I am strong I can erase tonight. Paul and I can still be together.

I let him lead me slowly back to the bedroom where I undress as he lies in bed, his back to me. As he reaches for the light, my panic starts again. I sit up on the side of my bed wondering if anyone will ever again really care about me, my moods, my dejectedness—but wait a minute, Paul has said he never really did anyway. I wander into the living room and sit silently in the dark, on our green couch. It's 3:00 A.M. Can I call somebody? Can I yell for help or must I sit here with a calm expression on my face and wait for daylight? Maybe I'll never sleep again. If I don't sleep then I'll have a nervous breakdown. If Paul doesn't love me, maybe I'll have a nervous breakdown.

I pick up the telephone and hold it in my lap. Its weight feels familiar and comforting in the dark. I'm not isolated and trapped here in this big box of my apartment with a man who may have temporarily or permanently stopped being my one true love—no, I can call John. I can call him at 3:00 A.M. in the name of emotional emergency. I am breathing deep long breaths, the kind you find yourself making when you wake quickly from a deep sleep. I dial and I wonder if I should turn on a light in the shadowy room, but it's too late, the phone is ringing. "Yeah," comes a gravelly voice. "It's Susan," I say, to my surprise in my ordinary voice. "Can you talk?" "Talk?" His voice is rumblier than before. "Are you kidding, doll? At this hour? Call me at nine and I'll be home. Goodnight, baby."

I pull the phone from my ear. Of course I have no rescuer. This one act symbolically and really proves to me that Schwartz and I are not meant to run off gloriously into the sunset.

I sit crying as each new thought hits me, waiting for the sun to rise. I am obsessed with Paul. What have we done? Is he rejecting me? Have I rejected him? What will I do next? Whenever we have a terrible fight my mood can go two ways. Either I can decide our relationship will be too imperfect—scarred and ugly—to continue into the future, that I deserve something better. Or else I can feel my facial expression go bland and adult, even find myself sitting straighter, and thinking nobody has a perfect relationship, and don't forget what you share with Paul. I love his walk, his smells, his laugh. Who could know me so well? Who could accept so much of me, who would be so intimate a part of my life for ten years? And who would be so smart about world events, life, and us? Who would tickle me from my eyes to my knees with his perceptions on books or movies or articles? And my writing. Would I ever write anyway without his support and pride in me—and his advice? I would be nothing without him. I should go make up.

Remember the time he cried when he had to tell me that my young cousin had died in a hunting accident. He cried that afternoon, rubbing his knuckles in his eyes with frustration, standing without touching me—wishing he could protect me from this, that he had the power to make it all a mistake, a non-fact. And I didn't have to cry then, because he was crying. I had to comfort him and make sure he didn't feel sad for too long. That's what marriage is, and it takes work.

In the past, Paul has usually been the one to make up after a fight. After I'd storm out into the kitchen, he'd wait a moment or so, walk past me, and start cleaning up the dishes. Trying to keep the trembling out of his voice, he'd engage me in some other conversation, often about a work problem of mine. Now I propel myself back into the bedroom. I stare at him in our bed, and I sigh involuntarily over and over. "Honey, take off your coat and come to sleep," he says, turning his head toward me. I am startled that he is awake.

"Paul, I love you," I burst out, counting the years on my fingers, my mind spinning out theories. "We've been married six years. We've known each other ten years. That's what love is, not some infatuation with a rock player or some flash across your stomach when James Dean soul-kissed Natalie Wood in the movies when you were sixteen. I think we can be all right."

"I think so too. I just have to be able to see Emily. You can't make me stop seeing Emily," he says stoutly.

This make me furious. My moods change so fast that I am surprised by each remark that I make. "I had an affair, too, you know," I declare, my face hot. "I slept with some-body, too, John Schwartz." He sits up in the dark, a rustle of sheets and a sigh. He walks over to me and pats my back over and over. "That's good dear. See, you can do things on your own too. Now let's get to sleep. You have to write tomorrow."

This time I take off my coat and I lie down in bed still wearing my polo shirt and dungarees. Since college, sleeping in my clothes has always seemed like a secret pleasure. Every once in a while after studying till sunrise or after a late-night talk binge with a friend, I would glory in the forbidden act. Now I lie in bed in my clothes, hoping to trick myself to get to sleep, though my head is pounding. He doesn't even care that I slept with someone else. The old jealousy is gone. He just worries that I'll be helpless without him. I'll show him.

At 5:00 A.M. I wake up, still lying on top of the covers to see him looking at me. "Let's just say that last night was a lot of unreality." He nods solemnly. In my relief at his words, a large chunk of anger leaps into my head. He wasn't even mad that I slept with John. Our sexual relationship, our private world is going to be like a broken vase, covered with the veins of old cracks. What is the use of it? I'd rather be alone or start all over again.

I sit up in bed, fuzzy and angry. He wants to see Emily. He said he loves her more than me. My sleepiness is dissipated by rage. I pat his bare shoulders. "Paul, it's probably too late. I just want you to have a good life." I am victorious. I can still hurt him. He tightens his mouth and walks to the bathroom. I am alone. When I said, "Have a good life, Paul," I really got him. I got him with that one.

May 22

I was just now opening kitchen cabinets searching for something to eat, I forget what. It's 9:00 A.M. and I have been avoiding the bed because Paul is still in it, and I feel that war has been declared. I can't lie down next to him in a tense parody of our old intimacy. Just as I tell myself I will survive—things will be all right—I remember that last night he said that Emily was more fun to make love to than I am. I grip the edge of the sink and stare at the drain for about ten minutes at yesterday's cabbage soup. I have to understand what is happening in my life. Paul and I did not have an all-night conversation, we had a final double monologue.

If someone could put a tape recorder into my brain, they would hear the screams of a deserted child determined to drive herself further into hysteria. They might also hear the adult in me whispering that if half the marriages in this country end in divorce, a lot of people have felt this bad. But how come no one told me that this gagging feeling was part of the white gown and till death do us part package? Till divorce

do us part would be more like it. But now I have worked myself back to my childish grief again. Divorce? I wasn't meant
to be a divorced person.

Will my panic about my future prevent me from sleeping?
My face aches so much from crying that the tears feel they're
coming from ducts in my cheeks and my eyes. If you don't
sleep, you have a nervous breakdown. I read that somewhere.
So I dial my psychiatrist's number on the phone. My voice
sounds so dignified, controlled. "I'm upset," I tell her quietly,
"I need sleeping pills." "Come get them," she says in her
cheery voice, no question, though I've never called to ask for
pills. We live in the same apartment building, so I can be inside her foyer in about five minutes. She is waving her prescription blank in the air to dry the ink. "What's the trouble?"
she asks cheerfully again. "Paul," I whisper, and the tears
come easily. "He's been having an affair with Emily, after all.
He says he loves her and I feel awful."

She wraps her arms around my shoulders and neck. My
eyes focus on her graying hairs a few inches from my face
at the nape of her neck. Her body is soft, but I don't relax
against her. This is another first in our therapeutic relationship. "It's going to be all right," she says firmly, enunciating
each word as though she believes I am suddenly slightly deaf.
If she's hugging me for therapeutic reasons, then she must
think I'm in drastic shape. I feel too tired to figure it out.

"I love you," she says in that same slow, precise, do-you-
hear-me voice. "Don't forget, I love you." She picks up my
chin, forcing me to look at her face. My hands rest uneasily
on her arms. "Do you believe me? I'm telling you it's going to
be all right."

I am embarrassed to be crying so piteously into her face
and I'm not sure I believe her, but I nod and wonder if she
thinks I'm the sort of person who could commit suicide because nobody loves her. Probably not, I reason, because she's
giving me the sleeping pills. Will I survive? I suddenly re-

member the horror I felt as a sophomore in college during the three-day Cuban missile crisis—when I first realized I could die. I could stop being me due to forces I couldn't control. I chain-smoked and sneaked out of the dormitory for a self-consciously romantic 4:00 A.M. walk through the dewy grass. But those days had a game-playing quality about them. Right now I'm not posing, I'm leading my one and only life.

So I stop crying and she is still watching me, her face a few inches from mine. Has she asked me a question that I haven't heard? As I step a few steps back out of her grasp, she says, "I said, get the prescription filled and I'll see you tomorrow as usual. And don't be too hard on yourself." On the elevator, I twist my hands together and sigh with relief. As long as I get sleep I will have the physical energy to brush my teeth in the morning. Then I am crying again, trying to freeze my face so the elevator man won't notice. What's the point of doing anything if Paul doesn't love me? Walking through the lobby in my coat over my short flannel nightgown, I am shuffling like a sixty-year-old woman. I can feel the lines of pain in my face like the creases of old age.

I don't go back home at once. I bang on Alice's back door and while she slips a tiny dress on her daughter, I tell her my news. She throws me a quick sad look as she drops the other sleeve of the child's dress. I'd hoped she'd pooh-pooh everything and tell me not to worry—again I wanted to be like the baby who confronts disillusion and then runs to its mother to have her lie it away. As her child struggles to put her arm in the dress herself, Alice sits on the floor. "You should probably see your shrink every day for the next few weeks," she pronounces. "You don't want to make a false move. Your marriage is in crisis and you are in crisis." So I slump a litle farther down into her kitchen chair for a few minutes before I walk up the back stairs to my kitchen and the scene of the war. Paul mercifully has left for school.

I seize the time to start typing notes feverishly; notes on

how I feel right now. Maybe I am a fool to be sitting here
by myself banging out these disjointed fragments. No. Writing
always makes me feel better. As each paragraph comes out
I watch it, judging it. Do I sound insane? Do I sound childish? I know my thoughts are caught in an obsessional spiral.
What is it? Does writing give me the illusion of control? I
know something is very different about me now. I am a walking catastrophe. I want to understand and to recover.

When the telephone rings, it reminds me that I haven't
called to get my sleeping pill prescription filled yet. "Hiya,
honey." It's Schwartz, guardedly cheerful, straining to hear
my mood in my voice. "How are *you?*" I mutter in a mockery
of polite discourse. "Uh oh," he teases nervously, "what's with
her majesty the Jewish princess today? Slept all night on a
pea, dearie?" His lightness sounds forced, especially through
the ten-second silence that follows. My mood lurches from
anger to indifference. He'd failed me by refusing to talk to
me on the telephone last night. "No, but I had a bad night
last night," I say. "Oh yeah?" he asks politely. "Yes, Paul
and I, well we had a fight and I guess he told me he's been
having an affair with Emily and he thinks he loves her." (He
thinks he loves her. What will bring me through this with my
sanity is the conviction that Paul is mad, not I.)

"Yeah," Schwartz is saying, "so that's why you called me
at 3:00 A.M. like a nut. You should've said something. I'd have
talked to you if I'd known what was wrong. Anyway, what
makes you think I was alone?" It is a graceful apology. But
I will accept no apologies. He wouldn't talk to me when I
needed him. I am too tired to even reproach him. Incredibly,
I feel angry and jealous about him, too. "If a person calls
another person at 3:00 A.M.," I begin a formal rebuke, "the
called person could assume it's an emergency." "Look, doll,
you didn't speak up. What am I supposed to be, a mind
reader?" I forget that I am supposed to answer him, so the

silence drags on until he asks, "What are you up to today?" "Nothing," I answer sullenly.

"Then why not come over and help me address envelopes for my upcoming intellectual-chic book party?" He is filing away at my unrested nerves. I'm in the middle of a big hole in my life, and all he wants is clerical help on his book party. My continuing silence warns him. "Look, baby, what's the problem? Your husband says he's found somebody to fuck and to love. You found me, right? I say you two are moving in parallel courses. A wonderful coincidence for all concerned, a mitzvah, dallinck."

No jokes for me. I erupt into a babbling fit. "Wrong. Paul says he's in love. I didn't fall in love." His silence confirms my words. Good, I hurt him, but I also cut myself off. I am making a lonely hiding place for myself.

But Schwartz won't give up. Because I am in crisis, he has decided to forgive me temporarily for rejecting him. "Dearie, I'll do the best I can for you," he starts again. There is a hint of formality, of good manners. "I wish somebody had done this for me when my wife and I split. For five days and five nights I thought I would go crazy or die."

Split? Paul and I will never split. What's he talking about? I want to rock back and forth and moan. But he's still talking. "Get your clothes on," he is instructing me, "and put on some makeup and come over here. Be a person. Believe me, I know. I been through it, doll. You feel like you don't have the energy to live through today, so you'll have to start faking it."

I agree to go to his house and hang up the phone. With one hand I hold my cold bare toes, with the other I clutch my stomach. Why don't I feel it's a wonderful coincidence that Paul and I have both chosen the same time to be unfaithful to each other with new partners? Why am I so jealous of him being with another woman, when I've had affairs now with two other men? Why does the idea of visualizing him lying on top of somebody else and sticking his penis inside her make me start to moan now to myself? And why does Schwartz's suggestion that I could be on my own terrify me so?

But this is getting me nowhere. I smooth my hair and retie my bathrobe. As I walk to the bedroom to dress, I wonder if I am afraid I am nothing without the label "middle-class nice wife." Am I afraid to admit to having negative feelings— that I want out—I want to reject my husband? What about my mental scenarios about kicking him out? Why am I so sure he's rejecting me? Why am I nervous about what people will think when they look at me at parties, or bump into me at the supermarket? I just don't want them to say, "She's the one whose husband left her. She thought they had a holy perfect marriage. She was delusional. She was smothering him and he dumped her. I bet she's a bitch. He's brilliant."

When a couple breaks up, I always notice that one gets credit for rejecting the other who then falls down and mourns the death of the relationship. One mourner, one victor. The victor is usually feeding on a temporary diet of narcissistic delight—loving his new sexual freedom. Why do couples so tidily divide their emotions? I guess it's partly based on where they are in their relationship. I am feeling vulnerable and want to lean on Paul. But he's as high on discovering the newness of Emily (I feel nauseated again) as I was on Schwartz three weeks ago—so I feel the loser, the bereft. And what will I tell people? Maybe I'll send out cards: "Susan D. Braudy wishes to announce that the one person who knew her best—her ugly and most private best—doesn't want to be with her anymore."

"He doesn't love me." I say now out loud, as I throw my bathrobe on the floor and look at myself in the mirror. I run my hands over my body feeling new bones at my hips; when your stomach contracts once every ten minutes or so, most food is out of the question. I touch my face with shaky fingers.

It's hard to believe I'm that pretty dark-haired person with round brown eyes that are only slightly frightened looking. If my looks matched my mood, my face would look like an old raisin.

He's become a stranger. Maybe he's gone mad. I get a spasm of a new fear. Instead of feeling shame and self-reproach, maybe I should be worrying about Paul's sanity. He spent last night rewriting our story. No more perfect couple. He now believes he married me only because he was lonely at graduate school. I remember the myth whose bits and pieces we'd blurted out to each other late at night or during long car rides over the years. The details that didn't fit, we conveniently forgot. We loved us. We were the girl and boy next door who got married, carefully smoothing over several odd boyfriends and girl friends as well as miles between our parents' homes.

I turn from the mirror, groping on the floor by my bed for my glasses. Maybe I should fight for my man. We haven't broken up yet. I can hang on. But don't I want some better deal out of life than a man who'd rather be with somebody else? I don't want to be a list of duties and outgrown commitments. But maybe I'm really just afraid to lose a fight for Paul. I don't want to play seductress. I'd rather not play most games. My psychiatrist says I often perceive defeat when none is there. As I slowly button my blouse, I sigh, conscious of the tangle of raw nerve endings and disjointed responses that make up me. How can I beg Paul to love me? Our love relationship is a "given"—how much can I fight for it? But hasn't the threat of losing it destroyed it anyway?

No, I want to hurt him by banishing him. If he cares anything at all about me, I want to show him I care less. So what if it's a lie? We're at war. I fear I could stop remembering to breathe in and out if I lose him. Still, I'll show him. He can still be hurt by me.

I feel like the hole in the earth after somebody's pulled

out the roots of a plant—barren, crumbled, no strong walls or boundaries—a shocked empty place that is full of pain and anger.

When I delivered the news last night that I'd had an affair, too, I'd hoped his stomach would ache as mine did every time he referred to Emily. Instead, he looked like a man who'd seconds before found religion in an orgasmic rush. "Paul," I hissed between clenched front teeth, "can you picture it, me fucking another man?" "No," he turned to me, his eyes teary and happy, "I can't picture it at all, Susan."

Noon

The back doorbell rings and I finish brushing my teeth before I answer it. Alice pats my arm and follows me into my bedroom to stare at me as I pull a belt through my pants. She is searching for positive things to say. "You really have learned how to put on makeup. It improves your looks and doesn't show at all," she announces while I smear rouge on my cheeks. When I don't answer, she recrosses a bare leg and peers at her sandals. "Look, he's an egomaniac, right? Maybe now you don't need him anymore, Susan. You've got your career. Remember that time you said you'd rather lose your marriage than your career? Was that just big talk?" I wrinkle my nose into the mirror. I know she is waiting for me to confirm her new rationalization for my life. "I like egomaniacs," I answer belligerently.

"Yeah?" she continues. "But marriage to one can be stifling. You aren't supposed to need a man around the house to prove you exist. You're the new woman." Her words are stilted. And I know she is putting on the kind of act you do for the bride's mother in the receiving line. You hope that everybody understands that your polite words are just meant to get you through events. I do remember a lot of brave talk as I explained my feminist conversion to Alice a year ago. But the phrases sound alien and abstract, right now.

As I look for my handbag, she stretches. "Buck up, if you want to you can find thirty men better than Paul." I am nettled by her dismissal of him. I say nothing, because I realize that anything would irritate me now. But how dumb does she think I am? I live with Paul for six years, and then we both agree he's a dime a dozen?

At Schwartz's house I dutifully flip the pages of the telephone book to the names of his literary cronies. As I address each envelope I am grinding my teeth in rhythm with my breath. Is this why I've been working so hard for ten years— so I can become some egomaniac New York writer's mistress-clerk? Paul never made me type papers or address envelopes. Don't think about that, just write the addresses and say nothing. Schwartz keeps stealing looks at me without, I must say, a great deal of affection. I am a curiosity, a good story he's preparing to tell somebody else. He doesn't want to come near me. And I look furtively at the outlines of his lips, his crotch. The idea of sleeping with him makes me shiver with distaste.

May 23

This morning the telephone rang before I'd even realized that Paul had left for school without waking me. My caller was the editor who'd once offered me a writing job at *Newsweek*. I'd chosen to go to *Glamour* instead where I have more free time; I don't have to show up for work as long as I turn in a feature every month. The editor is a friend of John Schwartz's and I wonder if Schwartz told him to call me again, now that I am in crisis.

This morning the editor's voice is as seductive as people let themselves be about business in New York—which is very seductive, since New Yorkers are people who've migrated from other cities to sell their talents in the biggest marketplace there is. A psychiatrist once told me that his New York patients talk more about work and success than they do about sex.

"We can use you right now. And the trial period will be shorter, because I have more time free to train you than usual," the editor is saying softly, almost purring. "So you just march in here at the end of the week. We'll dig up a typewriter and a desk, and you're on."

The tension in my stomach muscles disappeared for a second. Someone wants me. This is one way to get over the feeling that I'm carrying something dead around on my shoulders. I'll distract myself by taking on weekly deadlines and workdays at *Newsweek*. "It's a deal," I mumble. *Newsweek* here I come. I shake my head over how fast my life is happening. I gulp down a sleeping pill and two glasses of water and crawl under the down comforter, to sleep away the day. Just as I'm about to fall asleep I jerk myself awake with the realization that I haven't eaten since yesterday morning. Eat, sleep, bathe, brush my teeth. I must keep order. So I unfurl the covers and in the kitchen I drink a glass of milk and fold a piece of bread in my mouth in the cold draft of the open refrigerator.

When Paul gets home at six I am sitting at the kitchen table trying to convince myself that I am awake. "Get dressed, honey," he says, casually reaching for a glass and turning on the spigot. "We are both invited to Emily's house for dinner to talk things over. She would've called you herself but she was a little scared." My rage wakes me up like a cold washrag on my face. "I'm not going. You go and have fun." I am doubly upset. In the past he has made these decisions for me, forcing me to face situations I fear. But this time I am going to stand up to him. "I think it's weird." I feel like I am shouting. "What's her husband think? No, don't tell me." I raise my hand in front of my face as though I expect him to hit me. "I'm starting a tryout at *Newsweek* and you better let me alone so I can perform.

He looks at me with pity. "Don't be mean, Susan," he says sadly, as though I've confirmed his most negative thoughts about me. "Emily really likes you. She has this fantasy that we should all be best friends, that you and I and her and her husband should go for a long vacation in the Virgin Islands together and work this whole thing out." I snort with anger. "Does she still like me after all the things you've told her about what's wrong with me?" I ask. "And anyway, group sex isn't my cup of tea, I prefer sneaking around and committing adultery in private. It's sexier." I am almost enjoying my barbs.

He smiles a superior smile. "She really likes you," his words tumble out. "Isn't it funny," he's thinking out loud now and I am curious about what he's going to say, "how compliments from a new person can turn you on?" I know what he means. When Schwartz told me I was a long-stemmed New York rose, I sneaked looks at myself in shop windows for weeks afterward. "No," I lie in a snappish, whiney voice, unwilling to acknowledge the wonderfulness of Emily's compliments, "I always value *your* compliments the most."

His face falls, but he follows me eagerly as I walk back into the bedroom and lower myself into the bed, closing my eyes as I burrow under the covers. I wish he would disappear. I can't stand these fake conversations where neither of us is saying what he really thinks. "I tell you Emily really likes you," he says sitting on the edge of the bed to pull off his boots. He's patting my leg under the covers, and I pull it away. "I'll tell her and her husband that you have too much work to do tonight, but maybe you'll come tomorrow. Good night, honey," and he kisses me a loud husbandly kiss on the small part of my head sticking out above the covers. "Yeah, you both can jump off a cliff hand in hand. I'm not coming."

"Poor Susan." Paul jumps away from me and starts walking out of the room. "You couldn't begin to understand. It's such a relief to be able to talk to someone like Emily about you and me. Although I must say, sometimes she and I worry that we won't have anything to talk about, once we finish talking about you and her husband, but we will."

I am crying again because he and Emily talk about me. But my thoughts are solidifying. Today, I'm not vacillating so drastically between my feelings of nostalgia for the perfect marriage and my anger. Paul's joyful remarks are focusing me into the angry present. Emily wants to be my friend. He believes her. He's crazy. Let them run off together and see how long they sit on top of the rainbow before Paul finds there are complaints he has about Emily he can't make to her, so he starts telling some other dazzled listener his troubles: "Poor Emily, I probably shouldn't have rushed into her arms so quickly after Susan." I know I am trying to be the cynic about his new love story. I suppose this means I must also be the cynic about my future love stories.

May 24

My mind is made up, or I decide to pretend it's set. I tell my psychiatrist: "I want him out of my apartment." Part of me is hoping that she'll tell me I'm still loved, that she'll say patiently, "This is just a temper tantrum. Be patient. He'll come to his senses, and so will you. Don't think of him as your possession, your puppet who has to behave according to your rules all the time." But she looks out her window, lights up a cigarette, and shifts in her chair and says, "Okay, big deal. Suggest a temporary separation. People do it all the time."

Back in the apartment, I dial the Normandy Hotel, a respectable residential hotel about four blocks away, ask the rates and make a reservation in Paul's name. I make the call for two reasons. First, I don't think it's fair to ask Paul to leave his house without making sure he'll be okay. Second, I get perverse pleasure making the arrangements for him, knowing full well that he grabs the job of coping away from me under most circumstances (buying plane tickets, choosing vacation time, even demanding final veto over household purchases like a sewing machine or refrigerator).

I want to irritate him profoundly. He is swiping at me constantly, though he insists he doesn't want to hurt me. I will play his game. I too will pretend goodwill. So I call him at the office. "Hiya, honey," he said with boisterous good cheer. He's so crazy, he can't even express his anger. Maybe I am acting selfish, but he said he was in love. I want to hurt him. He should leave. I clench my teeth and neck muscles. "Paul, I want you out, out of the apartment." The fantasy was grounded. The words were now said aloud that I suddenly realize I must have been hearing in my head for a month while I pulled jam jars off supermarket shelves, washed dishes, or watched myself in the mirror brushing my teeth in the morning. "I want to be on my own." As I listen for his next words, I am overwhelmed with pity for him. I've gone too far. Poor Paul, the bitch has thrown him out, and he's only been as decent as always. "Oh, honey," he answers cheerfully, "thank you. You're doing this for me, because you know I don't have the nerve to leave on my own." And then my rage is on solid ground again. He is thanking me for kicking him out. He won't admit now that he ever cared for me. He's a changed person. "Good, dear," I answer. "I've made a reservation for you at the Normandy Hotel and you can call your friend Tim to find out if you could stay at his apartment. You have a choice." Wives know how to press their husbands' anger buttons instinctively. He got angry then. He'd masked any anger he'd felt over being asked to leave, but my arrangements exasperated him. In fact, as usual, he was now busy showing me what I'd done wrong.

"Well, dear, I think maybe you should be the one to leave the apartment, actually." His voice grows more eager as he analyzes our problem. "I mean, there's only one of you, but I may have all this new responsibility of Emily's kids and all. We need the space." I got the message, and it hurts. He's now dropped responsibility for me and assumed responsibility for three strange kids. But I answer neutrally. "Well, when the time comes, I'll certainly consider your situation, Paul. But right now, you go to your friend Tim's house or to the Normandy Hotel. Don't worry, it's near the subway to N.Y.U. You can have visitors, and there's a swimming pool—heated, I understand." "I'll choose my own hotel," he said. "Maybe it'll be the Normandy, but maybe it won't."

I am not so stupid about Paul as he is now claiming. Emily isn't the only one who understands him. He's pissed off, and if I want to piss him off more, I'll do a good job at *Newsweek*. I'll prove I don't need him to edit and push me to the typewriter and encourage me to write. Yet when I hang up the telephone, I am filled with dread. Every time I start to picture a part of my life or activities without him, I am convinced that I will not be able to function. I'll never be able to sit down at the typewriter in an empty house and write. But I shock myself out of my despair by saying out loud my psychiatrist's parting observation this morning: "Look, you know he feels deserted because he hasn't been your lifeline lately. If you have a breakdown, dear, he'll love you forever. Really, take my advice. Have a breakdown and the world's most competent psychic nurse will insist on returning to bathe your brow."

May 26

I wake up this morning and squint playfully through my eyelashes at the sunlight on my wall. Something terrible has happened, or have I just dreamed it? Is that part of a dream, too? It's the silence in the bedroom. Paul. He doesn't love me. And he's gone. We are "separated." I am separated.

I am crying without a sound because nobody will hear me anyway. I'm not getting up today. Why should I? Nobody gives a damn. And I don't either. I don't want to start moving my arms and legs outside my bed and act like me and start my day at all. How do people who live alone decide to do anything? Will I have a nervous breakdown? What is one anyway? Is it worse than this "who cares if I'm alive feeling" that I have today?

Today is the day Barbara is coming over to chat. She went to school with me, and now lives alone a few blocks away. She is a successful magazine editor and a good model for me. As people hear of my new situation, they call me. Nobody bothers me with questions that I have heard outsiders chewing over when they hear a couple has separated. Why did they separate? Is there another man? Is there another woman? Did he leave her? Why? Did she leave him? I sigh and start to fantasize a conversation between Barbara and Alice where the tacit assumption is that I am the loser because I've lost my husband.

Barbara wants to go to Bloomingdale's. I push the covers off me slowly. I don't want to go. So I call her and try to beg off. "I'm just too tired. I don't need anything, anyway. Some other time." I hear the coldness in my voice, but I know if I relax it might turn into a whine. "Susan," she is in charge, I am at her mercy, "it will do you good to get out. There are a few things I have to buy and you'll come, too."

After I'm dressed I walk to his closets and stare at his suits and shirts. They smell like him. I can picture him striding into the house unbuttoning the blue shirt and pulling off the red tie, or laughing in a taxicab wearing the heather tweed jacket with leather sleeve patches I'd bought him. Yesterday he'd packed some polo shirts, blankets, and towels into a suitcase and then walked out, his tie flopping, his footsteps jarring and heavy. When I heard his key in the lock again a few seconds later, I held my breath. But he only wanted to check the mail, which he did without returning to the bedroom where I was sitting in front of the television set trying to look at the strange patterns that were the evening news show.

Then the door slammed. I was "separated."

Now I start feeling around in the top drawer of his bureau where he keeps an old penny bank shaped like a pig, photographs of his bar mitzvah, and a yellowing Hebrew scroll, old credit cards, a Polaroid of an ugly red-haired nephew, and the keys to his parents' safe-deposit box. As I touch each object I ponder the historicity of this moment. His treasures are still here, in my power, in my possession—though he has flown the domestic coop. Flashback: a piece of his denunciation of four nights ago. Susan: "Don't you think I love you, Paul?" Paul: "Yes, but Emily loves all of me. You don't love a lot of things about me." Is he right? I do dislike the way he turns party crowds into audiences for his scholarly stories that I've already heard. But then I pick up the tiny pair of his baby shoes, cherished by his mother for twenty-some years, and then given to her son the college professor.

These shoes will be mine. I tie a neat little bow with each of the grayish laces. He is building a stepladder of generalizations so he can escape from me and run off with the love of his life. But he can't distort my history if I don't want him to. So I'll always possess his early marriage days in his twenties (I'm crying over lost fantasy). I stuff the shoes carefully in my underwear drawer. A souvenir of my six-year marriage. Doesn't this gesture make me pathetic? I don't care. I deserve an intact souvenir, and I'm quite capable of stealing it.

Barbara greets me lavishly. "You look wonderful, just wonderful. I love what you do to your hair, and you're slimmer, friend." I notice women flatter a woman who they assume has just lost a man. Joan Crawford did it in an old movie I watched last night on television while I drank a hot chocolate and lay on the huge, empty bed.

Alice rings the back doorbell and she and Barbara make polite conversation while I put on my winter coat. Barbara has blond hair, and with her freckles and pale skin and her trench coat missing a belt and two buttons, she could be a college kid who was a little distracted because she'd been studying all night for exams. She and Alice both went to Bryn Mawr the same time I did. But they haven't kept up a friendship. I watch them, two pretty young adults with long straight hair. In their early thirties, they've found a certain sophistication that comes with self-conscious efforts to achieve an upper middle-class life-style. They joke about Bendel sales prices, Kierkegaard, and a classmate who ran off briefly with a native chief whose tribe she'd been studying in Nepal. I don't really listen; I am still wondering why people must compliment the newly alone woman on her looks. A bell rings in my head. Why are you evolving a theory to put yourself down? Maybe you just do look very good right now. Maybe once they're single again women begin to take care of themselves better. Maybe they lose weight and start grooming themselves a bit better during these periods, to start sending out "I'm available" rays to men.

At Bloomingdale's, Barbara keeps up a barrage of pleasantries—stopping at counters to hold sweaters up against herself and then me. "You're so lucky you're tall, you can wear anything." "That's not true," I answer. "I can't wear things that emphasize hips. Now I'm a little skinnier, but usually my hips are a little too large." "You're hallucinating if you believe that for one minute," she insists, intent on pleasing me. "Men like curves, you know." I am soothed by looking at and fingering new objects. But I do consider my love of shopping a character flaw. If I were writing a fictional story of a spoiled contemporary Emma Bovary, I would give her my own personal passion for shopping.

I am suddenly rerunning one of Paul's denunciations from our all-night orgy of dismarriage. "All you like to do is shop, talk to your friends, eat in restaurants, and write. Emily and I have more interests in life. There are so many things we like to do that we could do together. We love the ocean and the beach. We love to travel to new places. We love parties. We love people and museums. You're a hermit, just like Emily's husband."

"Let's go to the lingerie department," says Barbara, pulling me by the hand onto the escalator. While we ride up I wonder if an amazing coincidence could have occurred. Could Paul have found another human being who shares all his interests? Over and over again that night he accused me of ignoring his work, his friends, his needs. "Emily likes to shop," I'd growled finally. "She shopped with me." "That's only because she likes you. She went along only because she thought you wanted her to. She always wears the same clothes. You know that." I sigh so hard that Barbara stops her chatter to stare at me. But why didn't I tell Paul that if Emily pretends to like shopping to please me, then maybe she's pretending to like museums to please him. If she'd work that act on me, maybe she'd work it on him, too. Anyway, there we are at the underwear and nightgown department. The counters are covered with pastel filmy garments, not the sort of things I wear.

I pat a delicate yellow bikini underpants, bra, and slip set. My own underpants are sensible cotton. Barbara is waving a black chiffon nightgown in front of me. "It's you. Let me buy you this nightgown and those yellow pants as a gift?" "No, no, I could never wear them. I wear flannel nightgowns or Paul's undershirts."

But if I'm going to *Newsweek* full-time I should buy an extra week's worth of underwear. If brushing my teeth feels meaningless right now, lugging my clothes down to our basement washing machines makes me want to go to sleep for a week.

"Listen, don't buy those." She pulls the cotton panties I've found out of my hands. "Like it or not, Susan," she purses her lips and wags her forefinger at me, "you're on the market again." She's still wagging her finger at me. "Look, at least you have something they value, so play it up, Susan, play it up." "What do you mean 'they value'?" I ask her sadly. "Men, Susan. At least you'll still have your looks for another ten years, so play them up." I can't bear the idea of being judged on my looks by men. She's setting up a series of tests that I can only fail. I can't start decorating my body at night to get new allure. But maybe something's wrong with me.

Flash: Paul told me that night that he loved Emily's perfume. "It's sexy," he'd said happily. But I can't wear it— some moralistic streak. I also would get tired of smelling the same smell all the time. "Later, Barbara, I just don't feel like sexy drawers right now," I tell her. "Susan, don't mope. Get angry. Think about what that schmuck has done to you. The other night I was at a party and some guy there from Columbia started saying that you'd kicked Paul out of this great apartment and he had to live in some seedy N.Y.U. housing."

"N.Y.U. housing?" I am shocked. "I thought Paul was at the Normandy Hotel." Apparently he got a big ugly apartment owned by N.Y.U. "Anyway, this guy was furious because you got this great apartment. So I told him off. I told him just how awful Paul had been to you, running around with that stupid woman right under your nose." "What?"

My pride is hurting me. The last thing I need is friends telling people how badly Paul humiliated me. "Listen, Barbara, he isn't so bad," I tell her intensely. "Anyway, I haven't exactly been home playing footsie with myself. I've had a few affairs, too, you know. Last September was the first and then I was actually involved when . . ."

"Susan, that's different. You didn't leave him over them, now did you? Anybody would be naive to assume that you didn't wander a bit. But you'd never hurt him the way he's hurt you. And he's out now having the time of his life. He's been appearing all over New York with her in public. Last night they were at your corner Szechuan restaurant with ten of your closest friends, a command supper by Paul to show off his new partner. I feel furious for you."

"No," and to my surprise my voice comes out clearly through the pain in my throat. "It's more complicated than that. You don't have to feel sorry for me. Honest." She pats my arm sadly. So I stop. If I keep going, I'll become the dirty adulteress, and she clearly prefers me as the woman wronged.

May 30

When my mother called last night, I lied to her. "How're things?" she asked, groping for the vocabulary to investigate my life. "Oh, fine," I answered, reaching for a magazine to flip through to make chatting less intense. "How's Paul doing? How's his book coming?" "He's fine. He's working hard." "Where is he, Sue?" interrupted my father on their extension phone. "How're you, Dad? He's at the movies."

They mustn't know. I've failed them. When the daughter doesn't have kids it's bad enough, but when the whole marriage breaks up it's a failure. Even so, it's not them I'm protecting by lying, it's me. I don't want their pity or reproach.

I don't need to step back into a child-role with them. They'll want to re-think my decisions, order me around, share my pain. I'm an adult now. I live in New York in an apartment and I am starting my job at *Newsweek* tomorrow. It's my life and I'm the only one leading it.

"What movie's he at, Sue?" "Oh, some Jerry Lewis movie at N.Y.U. Tomorrow I start my new job." "Oh, wonderful," my mother says vaguely. "Any other news?" "Nope." "Well, take care. It'd be nice to see you sometime." "Well, I'll be a little busy with the new job and all for the next month. It's a tryout so I gotta work hard." "Okay, take care, dear," and they're gone.

But they're not really gone. I married my mother's favorite young man. It's going to break her heart when she hears he's slipped away. I know we'll never discuss the particulars, just like we never discussed sex or religion. My mother handed me a series of illustrated booklets about sex when I was twelve. She had her "I'm uneasy so don't ask" look on her face. When I was eight and asked her if she believed in God, she got that strained look on her face and told me that it was her private business. Once I found a Tampax and asked her what it was. She got the same look on her face and said nothing. So that's why I knew Tampax had something to do with religion.

Once she came into the living room when I was fifteen and was talking to my friend June and her boyfriend. He was rubbing June's shoulder. My mother turned her mouth down and walked out. Later she told me, "I think it's poor manners the way those two were stimulating each other in our living room." That was it. And since it was poor manners to go on about the subject any further, she didn't. Once in a fit of anger when I was twenty-one and deciding again not to marry Paul one spring day, she lowered her face and glared at me and said, "Some people don't have to get married because they're taking all the benefits without any of the responsibil-

ities, aren't they, Susan?" I didn't answer her but felt her reproach, and didn't feel comfortable sleeping with Paul for
several weeks afterward.

May 31

I don't need an alarm clock to wake me at precisely 8:30
in the morning for my first day at *Newsweek*. I am so determined to function independently without Paul to wake up
with that I am out of bed and showered before the alarm goes
off.

At *Newsweek*, I quickly learn about my schedule for
weekly article deadlines. I have an editor to give me assign-
·ments. He'd promised to give me feature or colorful stories
before I was hired. I have an office with no windows and an
old gray metal desk with a battered Royal manual typewriter.
I have a blond, thin-lipped male office mate named Bill, from
Darien, Connecticut, who has five children pictured in several
frames on his gray metal desk. He gets an I'm-not-listening
look on his face after I get my third phone call at 10:15 from
yet another horrified friend who demands a summary of my
marriage status. Bill never takes off his tie and suit jacket,
although he is about my age. I watch him type a title caption
for a picture, his short hair tidily in place as his fingers fly
over the keyboard.

Maybe I'm the weird one. I'm that different woman I
used to read sad stories about in the *Ladies' Home Journal*
during the late fifties, the career woman without home, husband, or children, who really yearned for a loving if grouchy
"hubby" and dirty, rambunctious kids. The story was always
written through the eyes of a depressed housewife who meets
up with her old friend the glamorous career woman. Then,
after confessing a pang of jealousy, the housewife hears her

old school chum confess her own yearning for the hearth. So the housewife passes her crisis, and the bleak moment (a rarity in her life, we are told) is banished. You finished the story pitying the lonely woman who is at home in nightclubs, but has no family to go home to at night.

As I listen to Bill talking to his suburban wife by phone about kids' sneakers, private school applications, and Christmas vacation plans I wonder if there are short-story writers and clucking readers who would feel sorry for me. Bill has fulfilled the promises he made to teachers and relatives when he was growing up. He has become their sort of adult, responsible and bringing up the next generation. What will I contribute?

JUNE

June 25

I get up. I go to work at *Newsweek*. One office room, one corridor is my daytime horizon. I don't have time to think about Paul during the day.

Newsweek is an adult man's world, a successful, sober world of men. Like Bill they are clean-cut, high achievers who believe in playing the game to win. They have good teeth because they ate well as children and had good orthodontists. I've found them again, the guys who used to come to mixers when I was at Bryn Mawr. After college they went through a romantic phase, working perhaps as a London correspondent for a newspaper. Then after marriage came the high-paying spit-and-polish *Newsweek* career. At *Newsweek,* they moved up on the corporate ladder. They have good manners. They've learned how to write condensed paragraphs of lucid prose with topic sentences that lead the reader's eye from the last line of the preceding paragraph.

Newsweek is like a coed college dormitory. I am getting to know these men very fast, since everyone wants to talk to the new female writer. And since they are editor-writers cooped up in the office with nothing to do until the reporters' files come in on Thursday, they roam the hall sparring verbally with each other (impressive bouts—matches between word-smiths) and flirting with the females here.

Most of the male writers treat me with an uneasy—I suspect slightly sniggering—respect. They tell me I am the first woman to be hired from the outside as a writer. One reviewer came into my office to shake my hand and said, "Welcome to *Newsweek*. I wish we had someone like you in our department." For a second I thought he'd read my writing and admired it. "Like me? What do you mean?" I asked, uneasy as always about accepting compliments. "Of your gender, my dear. We need someone of your gender."

In the two weeks I've been here, the few wolves and heavy daters have already made themselves known to me. They are not romantic. They seem like decent people who have not reached for artistic dreams, though any one of them might have the writing ability to try to make novels or good nonfiction books. Instead they have chosen a safe desk, high salary, and daily schedule to fit their lives comfortably into. I don't want to get involved with any of them because my independent professional life is too important. At the office, I want to make it on my own. I don't want a male protector; a patron.

The women here are more complicated and more interesting than the men. They are brighter but much less sure of themselves. Like the men, they are the best and most privileged of their generation. Too restless to last for more than a year at graduate school in Cambridge, Massachusetts, or Oxford, England, they chose New York instead of marriage. And nearly all of them are working in subordinate jobs as researchers, reporters, or go-for secretaries under a male editor or writer. The *Newsweek* women are more obviously unhappy than the men. Many of them see psychiatrists. Since many of them are not married, they are anxious about this nonconformity. Today they are thirtyish, dress beautifully,

and are wedded to their careers and independence, though
they sound cranky and scared when they discuss why they are
not married or why they are not editors and writers at *Newsweek*.

I sense that they, like the men here, need the *Newsweek*
label. Back home, their parents know that even if there are
no grandchildren, their daughters have seen worldly success
because their names are printed on nearly one million mast-
heads every week. Though these women still dress and think
clean—no acid-heads or drunks at Friday-night office parties
—bitterness has crept into some of their faces in the form
of pursed lips and small furrows on foreheads. I am shocked
when they laugh about a writer who has been heavily rewritten by his editor. As is true for most people, life has not
rewarded *Newsweek* women amply enough. But unlike most,
they are smart enough to know it. They have no split-level
dream home in the suburbs. But there is no Bigelow on their
office floor either, because the corporate game they have
chosen to play doesn't reward women.

One mysterious facet of the *Newsweek* value system:
the reporter is a menial. In newspaper journalism the man or
woman who makes contact with the news event is glamorous,
transformed by the experience. Not here. The women who
have the pleasure of chatting with Woody Allen's mother,
James Taylor, and Senator Fulbright feel demeaned because
they don't have the privilege of writing the story. It is the
editor who runs the show. He stays cooped up all week until
the last of the reporters' files are in and then whips himself
into a fake frenzy of excitement to write *The Newsweek Story*.

The news magazine formula was developed by Henry
Luce for *Time* (always called Brand X in *Newsweek* cables
from the reporter, for example, "Brand X has sent out my
opposite number to investigate the Holy Roller phenomenon
in Seattle, so watch out."). Despite the competition between
Time and *Newsweek*—measured in advertising pages and

copies sold—many of the top brass at *Newsweek* were once employed by *Time*. In fact, one writer, the most unconventional of the set, switched back and forth twice, and his former wife still is a *Time* researcher.

Henry Luce's formula has several axioms. First: like any factory operation, a news event is better covered if the job is broken down into interchangeable parts. A team of people each contributes a piece of it. You have the six reporters scavenging their regions for stories. You have the researchers checking out the facts from afar. You have four editors in New York editing each other's editing.

Often, an editor will find a *New York Times* or an *Economist* story he wants to see in *Newsweek*. *Newsweek* doesn't break a lot of stories, but often covers them more thoroughly the second or third time around. So if *The New York Times* breaks the Pentagon papers story, *Newsweek* reporters discover the real identity of the man who released the papers and how long *Times* men labored over the story.

My first *Newsweek* story was my group sex piece. It was my editor's idea, and a safe one since it had been done in *Rolling Stone, Playboy,* and *Philadelphia Magazine*. I liked the idea of being the editor-writer of the story. And it was simply that some married PTA suburbanites around the country were organizing group encounters, with strict rules that kept them from being more than masturbatory tools to each other—no last names and secret meeting places.

I wrote a query cable about group sex to ten domestic reporters in ten different parts of the country. My editor edited my query to condense it slightly. Condensation is a vital *Newsweek* skill and done reverently. It is a skill I am determined to learn. The reporters had a field day with group sex. In Los Angeles one reporter got himself invited to a mansion rented from a movie star for an orgy. The stringer in North Carolina investigated the gay purveyor of group sex magazines. And a Midwestern reporter grilled the writer who'd written the best-selling lurid book about the new Middle-American phenomenon.

In a week, I had over 60 pages of reporters' copy on the subject. At *Newsweek,* you are told before you start an article how many magazine lines it should be. You then write them. After I finished the piece of 215 lines I took it down to the copy desk where it was "blued," mimeographed on blue paper and sent to various editors.

After several breathless calls last night from *Newsweek* reporters around the country—pleading with me not to leave out items like the woman with the big tits who claimed she dragged her reluctant husband to a group grope every week —it hit me. In a traditional newspaper sense, I was aborting these reporters. They were excited by having witnessed news events, and now I was writing their stories. The momentum of energy that a reporter brings to the writing stage is invaluable and makes newspaper journalism occasionally art. I was forced to whip myself into enthusiasm. I had witnessed none of the events I was writing about. But I had to pace my office and think of adjectives and exciting verbs that would convey the reporter's excitement. It was a great exercise in the *technique* of journalism, milked of the real passion of the city room and of reality.

Once I finished the story, my editor set his pencil to it. It knocked me out to watch him in his huge office with thick carpets, curvy modern desk, and ten sharp yellow pencils— each cast aside after he wore down the point. He, too, worked in his shirt, jacket, and tie. My romantic vision of a newsman, enhanced a bit too much from the movies, was that of a hard-drinking, roistering guy who chewed a toothpick and who knew everybody in town from the mayor to the bum on the street and also knew how to get them talking. I don't know who my editor knew, but he never left the office.

What about me? Would I rather be a news reporter? How do I fit into the *Newsweek* corporation? I did not get great marks at college. I was bored. I only came to life when

I became a writer and a reporter independently tracking a story. Could I sit at a desk? Something tells me I don't care to kill myself to write 150 lines of *Newsweek* print a week forever. It's a sophisticated game at which a writer doesn't hunt and describe a news story, or express her or his own emotions, or even see most of the original idea in print. Your editors and their editors are always adding their input—fiddling, condensing your condensation. However, it is a good game to play when your emotional life is in chaos. I don't see how it can cut your heart out to lose, but in this situation, where competition is keen, it makes me feel good to have the clubby male editors drop into my office one after another and say tersely, "Good story, congratulations."

June 27

I am nervous about how the elevator men in my building are treating me now that I'm officially receiving men at my apartment. I think they reported me to the building's owner who sent me an eviction notice a week ago, claiming I was now an illegal tenant, since Paul has left. Our lease had been signed by Paul. I got a lawyer and he told them some legal mumbo-jumbo and nothing else has happened. But every once in a while my world tilts and I wonder if anything will feel normal again. Last night one elevator man winked at a friend of mine and said, "Ah, her husband's left her, but she's still a fine figure of a woman."

June 29

I hardly remember my adolescent courtships. Ten years ago, "dating" had a goal: I was seeking the perfect husband.

I believed he would love me, solve my problems, and give me respectability. Now, however, I'm confused, I guess I want to feel I'm attractive to men, but not because I'm just an attractive female in bikini underpants. Besides, I am angry about a conversation I overheard through my half-open kitchen door yesterday. Our neighbor was earnestly telling Alice, "Susan will have another man to lean on in a month. She's too dependent to be on her own."

I enjoyed seeing Schwartz when I was a married woman. In a perverse way, it was easier. I wasn't measuring him against dozens of complex standards. Is he generous? Does he like women? Does he flirt too much? Does he like me enough? But now that I'm single, even his testimony on any of these subjects is not enough; I am constantly watching his body gestures, his eye movements. He fails my tests. He calls me at *Newsweek,* asking me to run errands. Will I read him a clipping from the morgue file? Will I have dinner with him tonight and pick up sandwiches on the way over? Why don't I cook dinner on Friday? I am thinking that sleeping with him while I was married was my attempt to make a friend without Paul's help. I was also reaching for something I had never sought before in my life—variety in sexual experience. Sex had stopped being a wonderful adventure with Paul. I guess I had hoped it was like that for all married couples.

Last night John asked me to meet him at a Mexican restaurant near his house. As I entered the dark small space, he was tapping the table irritably with both thumbs, making the candle flicker wildly. I hung up my coat and walked over to his table, impulsively kissing the top of his head. He straightened his tie impatiently. "Where've you been, sweetie? Now that you're a bigshot *Newsweek* writer, you don't even apologize for being twenty minutes late." "I thought you said seven-thirty," I answered. "I did say seven-thirty, dollface, and it's now nearly eight." "Oh, I guess the clock I checked was slow." "What?" His voice was rising. "You don't even wear a watch? Listen, in Manhattan, where people make six appointments—I guess I should say some adult people make six appointments—a day, only a baby would go without a watch."

I opened the menu to escape his barbs. He was watching me angrily in the candlelight. Then he went on to another tack. "And look at the way you're sitting. You are all hunched over like a schlump. All right, you've had a little tragedy in your life, or so you keep saying. But is that any reason for you to drag around like you're an arthritic eighty-year-old humpback? Some people are bad company when they're in misery."

"What's the matter with you tonight?" I asked, closing the menu. I couldn't believe that this man hating me across the table was one of the reasons I'd jeopardized my marriage. It's part of some great joke at my expense. I am some judge of character. Maybe he hates all women. "I have two things to tell you and you better listen to me and listen carefully," he leaned over to whisper to me, "because nobody is going to care enough or have brains and nerve enough to tell you again in your whole life." He was tapping his menu as hard as he could against the side of the rocking table. "First, don't get involved with another selfish careerist like me or your husband again. You're the kind of restless angry bitch who feels worthless and impotent so she attaches herself to a strong, ambitious man. But you get tired of living in reflected glory. You want some of the action, too. So you start competing and then he starts getting threatened, and he winds up hating you, sweetie."

He certainly got the facts straight. Should I try on his words, I wondered, and see how much they hurt me? Wait a minute, why's he telling me this now? "Look," I started to say, determined not to cry in front of him. Lately, I cry often when I am alone. I reached across the table for his hand, and spilled the ketchup bottle. "Look at you," he laughed loud, "you can't even play a love scene without twisting it like Elaine May. You're hopeless."

"You're just angry because I was late working at *Newsweek*. You're the jealous one," I was accusing him to shift the blame for the quarrel. "I don't have to put up with this."

"No, honey, you don't and you won't much longer. You know why? I'll tell you why. Women, passive women like you, use people to get themselves out of situations. You didn't want to hang around with that boring drip of a husband anymore, so you dangled yourself in front of me and I bit. Now you can tell yourself you didn't do anything wrong. Your husband fell for Emily. And I seduced you. You can blame the whole thing on me and your husband and feel sorry for yourself as a victim of circumstances. You'll never have to take any responsibility for what you did. And soon you'll drop me and blame me for it because I've served my purpose. People rarely stick with the person they've been fucking when the marriage breaks up. Don't worry, I know the game well."

The waiter had been standing a foot from our table, enjoying the angry looks on our faces and the tense sounds of our words. "Oh, just order some enchiladas so I can get the hell out of here," Schwartz said, closing his menu. Later, I will replay his indictment in my mind and sort out which accusations are true. Maybe he's right. Maybe I should find some less ambitious man. Maybe I shouldn't be with a man at all.

After twenty minutes of silently swallowing my enchiladas and then a quick cab ride home, I lie in my bed and cry to myself. I am truly alone. I know he was feeling sorry for himself, but right now Schwartz feels too nasty for me to spend a lot of time with. I have bought a new FM radio—one way I fantasize that people end their day gracefully when they are alone. At night I listen to WBAI, a listener-sponsored radio station. They play good Dylan music about this hour and the announcer sounds like the kind of smart eccentric I'd like to meet. I blow my nose and reach for the light as he describes his next guest, Jill Johnston. Boy, I'd love to write a long article about her. What a great idea: she calls herself a lesbian feminist and she tells all with wit.

I put my hand over my mouth, surprising myself. Lately I am noticing which gestures I still make when I am alone with no one to see me and which ones I don't. When I hit my toe on a chair leg, I never say ouch. I inhale with a hissing noise or jump silently around in pain.

As I turn out my light I have a smile on my face. That's one thing I rarely do lately when I'm alone—smile.

JULY

July 10

I have to admit something. Until last year, I preferred not to look at my marriage. Upon hearing of divorces or separations of friends, I would feel twinges of pain and doubt. But I avoided examining my own feelings and belief in an institution I had made my own. Like most people I had no way of comparing our shared private life with anyone else's. It was easier just to see us as living our parts in the "myth," rather than examine any specifics.

I guess a major problem is that our sex life during marriage went unexamined. We were simply embarrassed to talk about sex. Although Alice joked to me about her sex life, I never mentioned ours to her. I thought it was a betrayal. Once during a depressing job hunt I had not wanted to have sex for several weeks. Finally, after several fumbling attempts by my husband exposed my mute lack of interest, he said to me harshly, "Sex is not a very important part of life, is it?" He said that while driving in the country and with his eyes firmly on the road. I was too afraid to answer him, thinking only that in some major way I'd failed. The last time I'd really talked about sex was probably about fifteen years before when I'd giggled over dirty jokes with my teen-age girl friends. Nobody ever told me that marital sex wasn't perfect. Nobody told me it was perfect either. I think I simply assumed that it would be for me, as it was for anyone who was happily married.

I must say sex was usually Paul's idea. I wouldn't have known how to make the first moves and I rarely wanted to. We never discussed it. Sometimes I'd felt wistful or angry that he didn't concentrate on kissing and stroking me as part of foreplay; but jokes on television and movies showed me that other married people occasionally got these flashes of loss.

If we were awkward when it came to talking about sex, we still took tender care of each other. When either of us was sick, we got special attention—an aspirin in the middle of the night or hot compresses. Last night I felt sorrier than ever for myself when I woke up at 3:00 A.M. with a splitting headache. I have no special man to share my pleasure or my pain.

July 20

Two weeks ago Paul reappeared to stuff the last of his shirts and trousers into a heavy leather suitcase. I sat in the kitchen and pretended I was involved in my solitary breakfast. First water, then protein (my egg), and then my Vitamins C and Multiple arranged in a row. I wanted to scream into the bedroom, "Who needs you? Look how I've arranged my life. I buy my own vitamins now. I never forget to take them." But I kept quiet, pretending I didn't know that he was in the house.

Then yesterday morning I let him in the front door, demanded his key, and left him as he was packing books in supermarket cartons. Last night when I got home I ran my fingers over my disorderly, near-empty shelves and felt as though somebody I had once trusted had torn my clothes off in long strips. He also left a mess scattered around his study. I have to call him. On the floor, face down, is a framed portrait I'd painted of him when we were graduate students. Around his uncombed black curls I'd painted orange butterflies circling him like he was a luscious honeypot. I remember how he argued over the hairline, insisting that his was lower than I'd painted it. Next to the picture is a souvenir program from his senior high school prom—1959. I remember that night. We were both there, but with different dates, and I wished and wished I had been dancing with him. I wore my draped chiffon dress with a wide skirt to simulate hips. His date wore a clingy black sheath that plunged to show her fleshy chest. She whispered to me in front of the ladies' room mirror, without taking her eyes off her face, "Paul may be brilliant but he wants to get laid like anybody else." I was embarrassed and pretended I didn't hear her, wishing I was as pretty as she was so Paul would ask me to proms.

Tonight, he has just called to announce nervously that he wants to come and claim the phonograph equipment. "I have to think it over," I answer formally, playing for time. "Well, anyway, I want my records," he persists. "Oh yeah, well just let me see them before you steal away. I'm sure you took some of my books." My voice is rising. "You think since you're the professor, you're the only one who reads?" "Okay, honey, okay." He sounds like he's trying not to shout at me. "Okay, we'll wait."

I am so sad talking to him. Is he still hating me? I don't want to ask him about it, since I can't even face a cleaned up version of his new picture of me. "Let's have lunch," he says, changing the subject. "Maybe," I answer. Lunch, like we're two literary cohorts. Wait, I know why he wants to have lunch. A friend told me that Emily lunches with her husband once a week. Well I don't want to be a minor facet of their domestic arrangement. "Aah, I forgot, I have to hang up, Paul," I say apologetically. I hope he gets the message. I have more important things to do than listen to every sound he makes, hoping for the sign that will prove he is in pain and misses me and loves me and remembers the way we promised we'd be to each other.

July 25

It's two months since Paul moved out, and I often feel it's just too hard to get out of bed in the morning and inflate myself into shape. Sometimes I wake up in the middle of the night in terror because I can't remember who I am or which character in my dream I am supposed to identify with. Anyway, one thing for sure, I have joined the dating culture. I am part of a large group of slightly jaded New Yorkers who look each other over appraisingly when they meet at parties, supermarkets, or airports. I never stare too long at a man who wears Gucci shoes. I hate to look at guys who hide behind hair and beards. I don't like to look at bald or matching handkerchief-and-tie men. I look away from Black men—I see contempt in their eyes. I find some gay men bewitchingly beautiful at first, but I lose interest in watching when I feel closed coldness toward me, like a pupil dilating against light. Best of all, I love to watch teen-age boys—their sweet mouths, clear faces, gentle eyes—curious and undisappointed. Maybe, I say to excuse myself, maybe this is because I was a teen-ager during the last stage of my life that I was looking men over.

I am meeting too many men too quickly. Maybe they sense my hunger to be attractive. I am wearing tighter and more brightly colored clothes than I did when I was married. I don't think I know how to flirt, unless flirting can be not looking at somebody when you can't think of anything but looking at them.

At the airport the other day, I was late for a trip to

Boston, so I asked a man to let me in line for the shuttle flight. I expected from the angry look on his face that he would say no. He had a vivid scar on his forehead, as though he'd been marked by a bolt of lightning in a cartoon. His body was on the beefy side of muscled, but his mouth was soft. His shortish hair and loose brown suit marked him as slightly more conservative than I. He'd probably eat Passover seder with his mother and aunts, disapprove of rock music, and worry that women were becoming too sexually free. As he creased his forehead and sternly looked me over, I thought he was going to refuse to let me in line because it wasn't fair to the people standing behind him.

Then he smiled. "Yes," he said, "it'll make me feel omnipotent for ten minutes." Then in Love Comic book fashion as we were walking across the airfield, he asked if he could sit beside me on the plane. Since the ground and sky were covered with fog, our plane was delayed and sat in the airport for an hour. We discovered that we both live on the upper West Side and that we enjoyed laughing at the man next to us glaring in disapproval because we were picking each other up. He turned out to be a pianist about to leave for a European tour, and he recommended records I'd enjoy by younger concert artists. Finally the Captain announced that our plane would not fly; the Boston airport was closed.

But we'd made an understanding to stick together for the trip. In the airport waiting room again, each of us stood around while the other called Boston to say we'd be delayed. Then we shared a cab back into Manhattan to catch the Boston train. We spent seven hours on the train. First we discussed our favorite philosophers. Then he confessed that his Boston lady friend wanted a deeper relationship than he, who was wedded to his career of world tours and days of practice sessions. I told him about my marriage breakup and how sad I was feeling. Somewhere between New Haven and Boston, he asked if he could kiss me. I nodded, and we kissed. I closed my eyes at the sharp looks from the two businessmen in front of us. After fond farewells and an exchange of telephone numbers in the Boston station, I felt exhausted and elated.

"Hey cutie, going my way?" and I felt a hand on my arm. It was a long-haired boy of about twenty with glittering teary eyes who was sitting near us on the train. "I mean, why not try somebody younger." His voice was insolent. My heart started beating fast and my face froze. If I don't see you, you don't exist, I thought. "Come on," he said, falling into step with me, "you like me better than old scarface, don't you?" I spotted the ladies' room and after giving him my most disgusted look, I pushed my way into the crowd of women waiting in lines for the toilets.

AUGUST

August 10

The pianist I met two weeks ago called me at midnight to reproach me for not returning five telephone calls. I didn't feel the need to get to know him back here in New York. He came over. He kept saying, "Let's go to bed." Finally we did. I felt really embarrassed taking off my clothes in front of a strange man. Undressing is a necessity in these stiuations, I suppose, but I rarely do it even in front of women I've known for a long time. I was curious to see if I could be sexual so mechanically, but it was too athletic. Afterward he stared at the ceiling and said, "You are a sweet girl with a lot of love to give." I felt cranky. He was condescending. He was bulky in the dark. I wished he'd leave my bed.

I wonder if what I really want right now is "perpetual courtship." Men getting to know me in a pitch of sexual tension. Why then spend years or months afterward letting them into your life? Why mate? Why have prolonged intimacy with any man? O Freudian heresy. O watch my mother's full cupid's bow lips turn in on themselves and make a tight pink line of disapproval. "What about your old age, Susan?" she'd asked me years ago, contemptuous of my short-sighted pleasure goals. "When you're old, you'll be lonely. Sorry you never married." I'd feel a flurry of tension at her words.

Mother said when all else fails, balance present pleasure against that safe future. It was the sting of fear that convinced me that her words were true. Maybe I gave up six years of pleasure—the supreme pleasure of the courtship rituals, the chase, sex with strangers, and my own solitude—just to make sure that I would have somebody around when my body started to rot with old age. So what happened? Maybe Paul and I got tired of waiting for old age.

Sex with a stranger is pure sex. He is an unknown who has not angered you with unkept promises, hedged pledges, or the daily grind of watching him spit toothpaste into the sink, belch too loud, or forget to flush the toilet. I pledge no future after tonight except harmless fantasies of perfection— no past. The man as sex object, a person who cannot judge you.

It's new and overwhelming. Especially when one man has been your one and only everything. One and only sex mate. One and only husband. One and only male who says he loves you.

You can even have sex with two men in one day. Though I haven't, I get so eager for that tension, that pre-sex-act tension. Will I or won't I shock myself, take off my clothes, and translate my curiosity and tenderness and the tightness of pleasure in my crotch to the hysterical rhythms of the sex act? Will we or won't we? Every tickle on my stomach brings reasons why I should not please myself this way. Hi Mom, you're lurking back there inventing the first reasons—nice girls don't. You say it's disgusting anyway. Then came Paul. I promised to be true to him.

Now the reasons are harder to pin down. Remember I don't want to be a conquest. I'll be used. I'm scared to look at this male without his identifying turtleneck or dungarees on. Who wants to see the fold of fat across his belly, the brown-pink vulnerability of his balls? But after he touches me, and the sensations start, the reasons for not making love slip away. I am discovering how much I can enjoy sex. Sometimes I think I'll do anything to keep the feeling going. It's two brown velvet ribbons rubbing each other over and over. A penis wet is smoother than brown velvet. I feel like I am two pieces of brown velvet rubbing each other. I am the sound the two velvets could make, like horsehair rubbing on a violin string. My body feels like it is only my sex organs. And I become the feeling and sound and rhythm of sex everywhere.

August 30

I am a debased version of my old self. My parents and Paul always made rules against sexual encounters. I still haven't told my parents Paul and I are separated. There is no one whose rules I have to live up to now. This aimless freedom is heady and terrifying and I guess I have to find rules inside myself. Who cares what I do? I have to account to no one except myself. But I find it impossible to locate my self, my rules, so I guess I'll experiment. I am not the person I was brought up to be.

When I was a child, one of my older cousins, a female schoolteacher, about twenty-two, received a bouquet of roses from a man in Paris on her birthday. I remember my parents' disgust. The possibility that my unmarried cousin had taken pleasure in what seemed to have been a close friendship and possibly a sexual relationship was never mentioned. We were all somehow ashamed by this overt act of flower-sending which did not include a dignifying marriage proposal.

These days I am easily confused or hurt. Whom should I sleep with? What is casual sex? The question has been posed for me when old male friends suddenly appear at my doorstep and say, Why not? How am I supposed to respond? I yearn for some equivalent of the paper cigar band Paul slipped on my finger when we first slept together ten years ago. Then I try to tell myself again that I get as much pleasure out of sex as do men.

I enjoy the idea that men find me attractive, but I think the actual idea of conquest is a reflexively masculine pleasure. And I feel ill-used if I think of myself as the object of such aggressive motives. For example, after I slept with Andy last week (he's a trumpet player I've known since college days), he said, "You will always be to me what you are now, no more and no less." I felt tricked. I thought he was saying that our emotional relationship would never develop, that we could never be more than old friends and occasional sex partners. I am angry with him, and don't want to answer his postcard.

I don't like any limitation on the relationship imposed by a man. I try to convince myself that right now I don't want a lasting intimate relationship. Who knows what I will think in five years. Right now I enjoy my solitude. I believe (perhaps defensively) that I have proved I can live in a close relationship with a man, and currently I am trying to prove something else. But I am also disappointed in my failure to be a wife. And it seems important now to prove that I *can* sleep with anyone I choose to. Simply because for so many years I assumed my husband would be the only sex partner I would ever have.

SEPTEMBER

September 1

Yesterday I hailed a cab in the rain; to my surprise somebody was already slouched into the seat. I stared into the round brown eyes of a beautiful boy. With his white-collared blue shirt, his navy blue blazer, and Waspy, well-boned face, he looked like a Scott Fitzgerald hero. Most dazzling was the combination of his round brown eyes and his curly blond hair. "It's all right. I told him to stop for you," he said, tossing his hair off his forehead as I stared at him. He straightened up from his slouch. "I just came out of the hospital," he explained in a soft Southern rush, staring straight ahead of him as people do when they meet casually while traveling together. "I fainted twice the other morning because I stayed up two nights straight in my darkroom developing the world's most beautiful prints." He ended each sentence on a slightly higher pitch, so his words sounded slightly questioning. His desire to speak so intimately made me uneasy. I was not sure I wanted to involve myself by answering him. He gulped and grinned, forcing me to look at him. My God, dimples too. For a fleeting second I resented his overwhelming beauty. "You must think I'm real weird just going on like this." He extended his hand, lowering his eyebrows with mock seriousness. "I'm James Phillips the third and I'm talking too much. I feel lonely. What's your name?" I told him my name formally, wondering in my new appraising way if he was over twenty-two and hoping he wasn't gay because he was such a beautiful English tea rose of a young man.

After a silence, I felt him peering at me, so I asked politely what he did. City planning, which he studied at Yale. "When did you graduate?" I asked him, feeling like a lecherous older woman. "Last June." I hoped he meant from graduate school. I blurted, "I know a lot of people from Yale," forgetting my reticence in my surprise that we'd been part of a smaller community. He whistled. "Boy, it sure is some small world. What are you doing here?" I mentioned *Newsweek.* "Gee, this is my corner." He looked out my window leaning across me. I was jolted by how sensuous his mouth looked a few inches from my face. I held my breath until he leaned back. He was saying, "Hey, well, I mean maybe sometime somebody at *Newsweek* would like to look at my photographs. Sit still now," he continued as he stepped over me to get out of the cab. For a second I was sitting between his legs, then the cab was empty without him. The raindrops flattened his hair as he fumbled in his pocket for some change. Unfolded from the corner of the cab, he was tall, about 6'3", and just beginning to fill out his boyish leanness. He leaned over to stare into the cab, uncertain how to say good-bye. "Well," I said frantically, "come see me at *Newsweek.* We can talk about your pictures or just talk. . . ." He straightened up and his face was relieved and smiling. "You know what? Meeting you has made my day. Catch you later."

His day. I felt as though the ready supply of tears behind my eyes had evaporated. I squeezed myself into my corner of the cab, imitating James's slump. But he's just a kid. Boy, would Paul laugh. A former student practically. Am I so domineering that I have to take up with boys? But even my

best attempts to make myself miserable couldn't destroy the
half-smile that my face kept tightening into as I drove in the
rain.

September 3

James came swaggering into my office today, full of col-
legiate self-confidence. He told me of mutual Yale friends and
looked unblinkingly into my eyes. I looked away first. Perhaps
I was acting stuffy, given how attractive he is to me, but I
feared making a fool of myself. I felt responsibility for the
situation since I am older. He was sitting on my radiator, one
long lean leg in glen-plaid pants crossed over the other. I
watched his fingers gently rolling his newspaper. "Maybe you
want to have lunch?" he asked, and smiled as though we'd
just shared a good joke. I explained that I was writing a piece
for deadline and couldn't get away. I was pleased to sound as
though I could take or leave this glorious vision lighting up my
office. I didn't need to lose myself in those bold looks of his,
though for a few seconds they blot out thoughts of work, articles, sounds from the hallway, or even pain about Paul. I'm
glad that my cluttered desk makes me appear to be a woman
who is not dying to laugh with him across lunch tables, touch
him in bed in the morning, find him in the streets during rush
hour, and hug him during sex.

I've been married so long that I forget what men please
me, so I should make no rules. Experiment. But I surprise myself that I find someone seven years younger than I am so
sexually appealing. Anthropologists define a patriarchy as a
society where older men can have sex with younger women,
but women are forbidden to go with younger men. Thus men
have an ever-increasing pool of women to choose from and

women have an ever-diminishing one. Am I tough enough to break this rule now?

To me, James is an exotic, an antidote to John Schwartz, a younger person who has been forbidden to me by convention. Two days ago I thought I had nothing to look forward to except better work habits, grayer hair, and a getting-used-to feeling about depression. Today I remember all the young Yale boys in jeans and heather sweaters with long hair, lean chinlines, and tight buttocks. They were not real to me then; just ghosts of my own teen-age years. Now James is part of my present and future. If I am having trouble getting used to the fact that I am a scared and lonely adult, well here is compensation, a friendship holding sexual promise with a boy who likes me and who looks like a young Robert Redford.

September 6

Paul telephones to ask if he can take me out to lunch on my birthday next week. "No," I say into the telephone. My sullen mumble is sharp contrast to his ebullience. I feel he is proving to me how pathetic I am to have lost the world's most perfect husband. I'd like to think of him as dead. Sometimes a mutual friend will shatter my protective illusion and say, "Oh, I had a Chinese dinner with Emily and Paul last night." Impossible, I usually think, Paul alive and well and smiling and giggling and looking out of the corner of his eye and dancing at parties and loving another woman? No, this is too painful a reality. I reject it. I can't bear it. I even want to avoid friends who keep seeing him. I have this joke with my friends: whenever they mention Paul, I pretend that I am Katharine Hepburn playing the noble widow, "Pardon, but are you talking about my late husband, rest his soul in peace?"

"The friends are the loot, Paul," I snarled at him on the phone the other day. And it's true. I feel we are in competition for our friends. He called me a hermit the night we broke up. I'm determined to show him. "Friends go with power," an ex-wife once told me. I'll show Paul that I'm not powerless. I am forcing my close friends to declare allegiance to me only.

My shrink is sarcastic about my dead-husband fantasy. "If you had lunch with him once a week . . ." "No." I stick my lower lip out. "Well, once every two weeks, then he'd become this nice male person you know who teaches at N.Y.U. and who can be helpful about writing and all sorts of book information." She sounds sane. But I know this will never happen. He is my failure. Not only did I renege on the one promise I'd always meant to keep—to stay faithfully married forever—but he broke his to me. "Anyway," I tell her as she watches me, "his lady friend keeps her husband on the string by having lunch every Monday. Monkey-see, monkey-do. He wants to have a spouse date, too."

So she makes her speech. I know it by now. She's trying to get me to admit I was tired of him. "That's it," she taunts me, "hug that rejected feeling to you. You'd walk a mile to make yourself miserable. Maybe he misses you. You aren't all that repulsive. He didn't reject you. You got each other to New York, then you got involved in journalism. You didn't need him anymore."

"Don't you think I loved him?" I ask tremulously, conscious that she dislikes the term love, because it's mystifying and self-indulgent. I am also conscious that I've used the past tense. "You 'loved' him when you were in trouble. Most of the time you kept him in the closet like a raincoat. When skies were sunny, dear, he stayed in the closet." I glare at her, unwilling to accept her definition of my selfish love. "He taught me how to love," I assert, my voice breaking, "how to care about somebody else's happiness as though it were your own.

I doubt I'll ever feel love like that again." After a silence, she says, "All the more reason to have lunch with him, no?"

Back in my office, I dial his number. Emily answers the phone, and my face flushes. Why can't he answer his own telephone? "Is Paul there?" She recognizes my voice and stumbles a little, "Aah, sure, wait a moment. How are you?" She rushes through the phrases like a scared kid. "Fine," I cut her off curtly.

As soon as he picks up the telephone, I blurt, "It's okay for lunch next week, if you still want to." It's not killing me to talk to him this time, and I wonder why. Then I remember. James likes me. Just the idea of a new man's attention makes Paul more remote. Paul is a little withdrawn. My good spirits affect him, the way his manic moods get me. We don't wish each other well.

September 13

When Paul enters my office door I am irritated by the way he looks. He has let his hair grow much longer, and it sticks out from his head in a flamboyant Afro so that you can see the white scalp between the hairs. I want to order him to get a haircut. "What's happened to your hair?" I ask instead. "Vidal Sassoon. Do you like it?" he asks, waggling his eyebrows with pride. There's a new energy about him, it starts with the rapid movements of his eyes. "Well, you look like you just got electrocuted," I answer, trying a hostile joke to mute my angry feelings. I notice he's wearing expensive ankle-high brown boots, the kind I'd always urged him to buy. "Oh, I see you finally stepped up to decent boots. How come?" I ask, slipping into my coat. He extends a foot pridefully. "Emily bought me these. You like them?"

He's telling me that Emily and he take care of each other

now, and he has forgotten my ideas on things—like boots, for instance. I feel miserable. Well, maybe he is different. He doesn't act like my Paul, who wouldn't strain like that to see his reflection in store windows. At the entrance to the Museum of Modern Art, he stops and shades his eyes to look at me. "You look good, real good." He beams at me. I push ahead of him into the crowd at the entrance to the Museum. Don't lie to me, I tell him silently. If I look so good, why the hell did you leave?

Inside the museum he walks up to the information counter to say he's a member who's left his card at home. "I don't have to pay, do I?" he asks the clerk. "What about me?" I ask the man. "Are you a member?" he asks me. Paul is wiping the front of a boot on his trouser leg. I know that as his wife I am a member, but should I assert this delicate fact? I wait for Paul. He's whistling to himself and says nothing. "Oh, I'll pay for you," he says expansively. After another half a minute, I say, "Oh wait, isn't it a family membership?" "Yeah," the clerk answers impatiently, looking over my shoulder at his next customer. "Well, I'm his wife. I guess I can get in free." My voice sounds shrill and I glance over to find Paul smiling sheepishly. "Well, why don't you say so?" The clerk is shaking his head with pretend amazement while he writes me a temporary admission ticket. He is relieved to be rid of us. I am humiliated; I've said the wrong thing, made an unwanted claim on the new bachelor.

Upstairs in the members' dining room, we are surrounded by Warhol and Lichtenstein posters, and by expensively dressed New Yorkers wiping their mouths carefully after each spoonful of vichyssoise. I fuss through the junk in my pocketbook for a cigarette. "I'll buy you a pack." He half-stands in his seat. "I can get my own." I struggle to my feet and to my surprise he's standing, too. We face each other over grapefruit and vichyssoise. "What's the matter," I ask, "have you become the gallant gentleman, fetching Emily's cigarettes? I can get my own. I don't need your help." He sits down and sighs in despair of me. "Get your own then. Actually I've decided to help Emily quit smoking. I've got her on to True cigarettes—low nicotine. And she's down to a quarter-pack a day."

I could murder him. "Oh yeah, when are you going to unblock her and get her photographing again, Paul. When are you going to pygmalionize 'poor Emily'?"

"I do have her photographing again. I made her a schedule," he answers happily. "And what happens if she's any good? Or don't you have to worry about that?" I say, curling my upper lip into the nastiest sneer I can make in such a civilized public room. "Or maybe, Paul, you won't be as competitive about a mate who's a photographer. You can be the only writer in the family." "Exactly," he laughs gaily. He thinks we're joking around. I'd like to kill him. "You're right," he is explaining, "I don't have to worry about her getting a slightly better shot of a violet than I can, now do I? So I won't have those problems this time."

As I walk with dignity to the cigarette machine I feel like a woman having a low-key breakdown in a *New Yorker* short story. I am celebrating my thirtieth birthday with my newly former husband, a history professor, in the Museum of Modern Art members-only dining room: all the success symbols are as perfect as a funeral floral arrangement. But I want my husband, not this foppish stranger sitting across from me, but my old friend Paul, loyal, bookish, helpful, always there. What is it that happened to him, to us? It's hard for me to remember. The genteel birthday luncheon, the graphics on the walls, and the small-talky conversation we must make now because the nasty banter was killing me—these are unreal. But they make the fact that I'm growing old and disappointed a little easier to deal with.

September 13: Evening

It's nine o'clock and still my birthday and I want to stop thinking. I dread taking one of those serious birthday looks at myself. I am alone on my floor at *Newsweek,* I enjoy the feeling that I'm working longer hours than anybody else. After writing a memo suggesting an article on Arthur Janov, the therapist who claims to cure patients by having them cry their way back to childhood pains, I write a few checks for doctor bills. Paul liked to control our joint checking account. I went to the bank very rarely during the last three years of our marriage and paid few bills. Bill paying is now one of the hardest things I do. I am ashamed that I still keep our joint account, but the idea of filling out forms with rules and tiny print gives me attacks of terror.

I felt insane the week Paul left when I first went to the bank on my own. My hand shook as I knocked over the neat pile of forms on the customer service counter. First I dropped the pen chained to the counter, then I dropped my change purse. As I squatted on the floor, picking pennies up from around people's shoes, the guard strolled over to me. "Anything wrong?" he'd asked. "I don't think so," I answered hopelessly.

Yesterday a fellow *Newsweek* writer listened sympathetically when I complained about paying bills on my own and instead of jeering, he said, "Look, I felt like that when my wife and I split up. Only I went on a six-month drunken binge before I assumed responsibility for my life. I have a tip. Make folders labeled bank, doctor, dentist, telephone, and miscellaneous and store your bills here in your desk and pay them on Mondays. We don't do anything around here Monday anyway." I am always surprised when I reveal a private fear only to discover that it's a common problem.

I close my file cabinet and think about my psychiatrist's latest pep talk, planning activities to make myself happy. Within seconds, I am dialing. When James answers in his sweet, questioning voice, I start talking fast. "I was just sitting by myself at work and trying to think what I'd really like to do, and I thought I'd really like to go for a walk along the park by my house. And it's really something that is done better with someone, so I'd like to do it with you." He takes a deep breath. "I'd sure like that."

For a while, until he figured out how old I was and what was going to happen between us, James was all eyes. It's not going to be easy, I thought, as he ducked his head toward me twice as though to kiss me after saying hello. There's something about his youth that made me feel it was awkward for him to be the one to decide to kiss.

Sex feels impossible before I do it for the first time with someone. I feel lost without commitments like Paul's cigar band. The rules have changed since I was a teen-ager. You now do it with a stranger as one means of deciding if you like him. But I know James likes me by the way he keeps staring at me out of the corner of his eye when I'm quiet and by the unblinking stares I get if I look at him.

At first I wondered if I could ever allow him to be in charge of our lovemaking. He kept trying to sweep me into his arms Rudolph Valentino-style. But then I remembered the moment he'd stepped over me to get out of the taxi-cab, how I'd wanted to watch him naked, and touch his hair as it bumped against his forehead while we made love. So our seduction scene was efficient, robust, no seduction at all. I had never felt lust and curiosity so keenly. And I had never dreamed it could be so quickly satisfied. When I was married, sex was something I remembered I liked after

I'd been making love for a minute. It had rarely been my idea
to make sexual advances. I'd always have an "Oh, yeah, well
I feel something I guess" response.

I put my glasses on to watch James sleep on top of my
sheets, a long, narrow body. I loved having sex with him.
I'm learning to take this pleasure for myself. After about five
minutes, he stretched his arms, his eyes still closed. "You know
what I think about when I make love?" "No." I watched him
closely. "Well, I say this crew cheer over and over that we
used to chant in prep school to keep us rowing together. Two-
four-six-eight, we-will-win-'cause-we-won't-wait. Sometimes I
say it two hundred times. It keeps my endurance up." His eyes
were still closed, his cheeks flushed with embarrassment, and
he was grinning. I patted his shoulder, touched. Then I started
to wonder what people think when they're having sex. Paul.
Suppose Paul chants to himself. Then I was irritable. How could
the great love of my life have thought about anything but love
and me during our sex act? Poor me, poor Paul. What impossible roles husbands and wives demand of each other. We
couldn't talk about sex because we couldn't live up to our
"perfect couple" image. We would have angered each other if
we'd confided our silly secrets. Paraphrasing the novelist
Richard Stern, no wonder more of the world was in our heads
than in our talk with each other.

OCTOBER

October 20

There is little surprise to James. After weeks I can read his nervous smiles, his eye movements. It is perhaps because I have lived through so many more events than he has. If Paul played the "gardener" and I was the drooping flower he had to take care of, then with James I am in charge. I am the gardener. I feel like Paul when I try to explain away his guilty moods. I try to tell him that he will one day laugh at the self-loathing he feels when he's around my older male friends who have eight years more worldly success than he does. He can't understand that he threatens older balding males, nor will he admit he feels insecure, but makes fun of them. He refuses to believe anything he has not experienced. In some moods I feel protective. In other moods I get impatient with his smaller perspective. Our relationship is not between equals, but it's important to me. I enjoy feeling stronger than I once did though sometimes I feel sorry that I'm not with somebody my own age who sees at least as many of life's nuances as I can.

October 30

My apartment seems larger since Paul left. Tonight I tell myself that alone is not lonely. Other nights I walk slowly through my apartment enjoying my solitude. I am learning to enjoy my own company. I am in charge of six rooms. However, I don't go into Paul's study; I pretend it isn't part of my house.

Friends sleep here often now: a steady stream of out-of-towners who unpack their suitcases in the maid's room and in the living room and who meet over Saturday breakfast. I feel the apartment has new room for them. I am opening up myself and my house to people.

I'm going to find a roommate to live here after a while. The space often feels too big for one person. And I sometimes get tired of congratulating myself on how adult I am to live alone. Sometimes right before I go to bed, I feel deserted. I need company. I'm not all that brave. But since I seem to get angry at, feel disappointed by, or run away from men, I will live with a woman.

October 31

I have noticed in myself new anger at men. If they joke about me or other women, if I let my work go and spend time with them, sooner or later I get flashes of anger. I get angry if they try to get close to me. I think I am also angry because of my unclear expectations. I married my teen-age fantasy, Prince Charming, who would take care of me and soothe my anxieties and make me lovable and beautiful. And now Prince Charming is gone.

Have such fantasies turned sour? Are women expecting less or more? Or are they just talking more openly about anger and frustration they have always felt? My prospective roommate's father asked her when she left her second husband, "Why? Why?" "I wasn't happy, Dad," she answered him. "Happy!" he exploded, relieved to find something besides himself to blame for her failures, "Happy? Who's happy? Who said you should expect to be happy?"

High expectations cause the most pain when we are disappointed. Low expectations make for easier satisfaction. I might not get so angry at a man I expected less from. I should expect to save myself—cure my anxieties, tend my own illnesses, and maybe learn to like myself a little more.

NOVEMBER

November 1

Once when I was in the third grade, Gary, a chubby-faced quiet kid who didn't read as well as I did, passed me a folded note. I opened it in my lap and read, "I love you Susan, very much." My whole body flushed as if I had lowered myself into a bath of warm water; and I looked over at Gary who was lost in thought, his finger slowly tracing a line in our lesson book. Who could have guessed that he cared for me? I was lovable, now that he loved me. Afraid to let a moment go by that would deprive him of the knowledge that I returned his feelings, I quickly tore a page from my composition book and wrote "I love you Gary," folded it and passed it to him. He opened it and then looked at me and shrugged his shoulders.

Confused, I looked around to see if anybody had noticed our illegal note passing. I caught sight of Bobby Young who sat on the other side of Gary's desk, folding a piece of paper and giggling as he whispered to Gary, "Pass this one on too." Gary shook his head no, perplexed and tired of passing papers from Bobby on to me. "Pass your own notes from now on," he whispered to Bobby. As for me, I was humiliated. How could I love Gary so easily by mistake?

I should have learned a valuable lesson. Love should be easily given and received. I, however, learned as a female to be inoperative, ungiving until a man gives me permission to love him by signaling that he loves me. I am afraid to be the seductress. I am scared to lose. Men can more easily afford to take chances—be the seducers, do emotional high wire feats—and me, I must manipulate the act with whatever off-stage or mystical powers one could summon (lipstick, perfume, gossip information, even hanging around unobtrusively). More important, I see the passivity carry over into my work life. I have been trained as a woman to be impotent and cursed with a certain inability to play the games of life. But I am also protected from some of the shame and catastrophe of losing, a chance that a Lothario, a Casanova always takes in love.

November 5

My friends force me to feel among the living. I am lucky New York City is one place where you don't have to be part of a couple to have a social life. Judith calls me on the phone to invite me to a dinner party at least twice a month. She also knows that even if I accept, I'll telephone her the day before and try to get out of it, saying I feel too tired or that I'm getting sick. But she cajoles and tricks me into coming anyway. I keep forgetting the reasons why I must put on my coat, get on a subway, greet her and several strangers, and settle down to an evening of formal chatter. I usually feel irritable because these encounters interrupt my self-absorbed thoughts about Paul and what has happened to me.

At first the evening is only a strain; I force myself to

smile and make polite noises while well-dressed strangers describe interesting gallery openings, trips to Spain, or problems with rent control. I keep hoping no one will ask me if I'm married. But then I start to be reminded of the superficial details of my life that might make polite conversation. I tell them about how my cat has taken to peeing in the kitchen if I don't get home at night in time to feed him. And finally I get a small sense that my mind is being slowly eased, as I realize I have spent several hours not rerunning fights with Paul or random news I've heard about how he's living his life now.

It's these civilized, formal events that my friends are ruthlessly pulling me into that will make me forget for longer periods of time that I am not carrying this dead or dying thing around on my back. It's my network of women friends who offer me the least predatory and most soothing relief. Sometimes I want to grab Judith's shoulder and say, "But I've failed. You know I have. And I'm so confused." She doesn't seem to care to judge me, so I know it's all in my head right now.

November 8

Once a part of marital society, yet now outside it, I am drawing confidences about flaws in marriages the way a straw draws up a milkshake. Yesterday Carol and I went out for late-morning coffee; she and I had gone to college together and proudly we find ourselves still stimulating and liking each other.

If we'd met today, Carol and I might not have become close friends. I am a devoted career woman and she runs a family of four boys, a parakeet, and a poodle without domestic help. As it is, we don't worry. I think we have settled on a tidy means of appreciating each other. I glow when one of the kids squeezes her cheeks and says, "My mommy is beautiful and I love her." She nods her head and gives me an honest if overpositive reaction to an article of mine that she's happened to read.

But now that I am separated, some taboo has been lifted between us. The publicness of my marriage problems makes privacy between us irrelevant. Carol listens to hours of my telephone talk about sex and loneliness. She even makes suggestions about my finances after hearing my repetitive budget worries. Then tonight, after she tricked her youngest child into staying in bed long enough to fall asleep, Carol told me a secret about her own marriage. Her husband runs an advertising business that requires him to go to Boston for long weekends. One day last July while he was away she was standing in line at the neighborhood butcher, when she struck up a conversation with a man who lives in her building. His wife and kids were away at the seashore. What could be wrong with combining dinner plans, she thought; with her kids throwing food around it was bound to be innocent. But one dinner led to another and to a kind of understanding.

Her husband's conversation is mostly accounting and advertising gossip. Her neighbor, newly in psychotherapy, speaks of his personal problems, observations of other people, and the need to feel love. Carol slept with him after their third dinner, and now she finds herself wishing that her life would fall into place: that his wife would again go away during one of her husband's Boston business trips. She and her lover have pledged to be casual and not risk anything in order to continue their passionate encounters. Only Carol tells me that she can't stop thinking about how white his stomach was compared to his suntan, how much they laughed when she toasted him in his bed and then spilled the sangria. "And I knew by the look in his eyes when I took off my dress that first time that he adored me. I thought, at last the tapestry of my life is complete—a man adores me." As she talked, she stood to look in the mirror above her sofa to smooth her hair. "Oh, my husband likes me okay, but he takes me pretty much for granted. I mean we never had a great passion between us, but we have mutual respect. You know what I mean."

I knew what she meant. And her narcissism and her pleasure in her affair annoyed me. She reminded me of Paul dancing with his earphones on in front of the mirror. I left early tonight; she had taken away my vision of another "perfect couple." Also, I am jealous, too, of that time in a marriage when a first romance gives you the false idea that men and sexual excitement are out there, waiting for you to plumb.

You don't have to worry about loneliness when the affair is over. In a way—momentarily anyway—you have combined security (your mate) and romantic fantasy (your new crush).

But Carol is only one of my friends who've confided in me recently. The most difficult ones to listen to are the husbands and wives married to each other. The wife of Allen, a colleague of Paul's said that her husband would never look at another woman. She'd been telling me about her own sexual infatuation. Allen is one of the several husbands who have proposed themselves to me recently for a casual affair.

DECEMBER

December 1

I woke up at 3:00 A.M., my knees stiff with tension. I can't do it, I said aloud. I can't spend my weekends for the next few months reporting about lesbians. It started with a short piece I wrote for *Newsweek* on Jill Johnston. I never saw her myself, but the reporter asked her questions I had sent him: "What do you hope to gain by telling everyone you are a lesbian?" "How are lesbians like other women?" "What was your first lesbian experience?" Then a week ago, I asked an editor at *Esquire* magazine if I could write a long profile of her.

December 2

I am writing about her because I am curious. Once a senior "beatnik" had looked into my sixteen-year-old eyes in a bathroom mirror at Girls High School. Then she told a friend of mine that I looked like a lesbian. I felt sick to my stomach. It started with my 5'9½" height. I was a freak. A few months later at the bus stop near my high school, a little old lady with stooped shoulders and an eye twitch poked me in the side and whispered, "If God wanted you to be a man, he'd have given you a penis. You may be tall, but you're not a man. Why are you wearing pants?"

Again I was sick. These incidents posed the overwhelming possibility that something was wrong with me, that I wasn't a real female. It had something to do with my shame at my mother's decision that I shouldn't wear high-heeled shoes because I'd be taller than all the guys I knew. If I was too tall to dress the way women did, maybe I was too masculine to be a woman at all.

Even earlier, before I entered high school, I remember sitting in a Howard Johnson's with my uncle and aunt and their two sons. After the waitress dumped glasses, napkins, and silver in a bunch, my uncle announced, "Susan will arrange the silver." "I don't know how," I answered, hearing that he assumed the job beneath himself and my male cousins. "You're perverted," my uncle said and my aunt said "shush" and gracefully pushed the spoons across the white tablecloth with small dainty fingers to their rightful places. "You want to be a lawyer when you grow up and you can't set a table," my uncle went on. "You're perverted."

Tonight I am upset about Jill Johnston—about something unarticulated, unknown. What will I learn about myself if I get to know this woman? A year ago, I dreamed at night of my old friend Judith touching my hand and looking into a mirror at me, and my muscles in my thighs pushed together with sexual feeling. I woke myself up in horror. Do I secretly long to have Judith touch me? We look a little alike, being the same height and all. Isn't homosexuality narcissistic? I know what would happen if she did touch me. I would become loathsome. I would have failed the most basic expectation of my parents, my teachers, even myself. Sometimes when she touches my hair or kisses my cheek, my skin tingles and I hold my breath waiting for the next physical sensation to prove what I so fear—that I am getting turned on. So far it hasn't happened.

But do I want to meet Jill Johnston and her friends to test it still further? No, I don't. But on the other hand, it's a great article. Jill Johnston's expressiveness about her sexuality is part of the new climate now. As a journalist, I know she is part of the current emotional mood and perhaps a harbinger of a new order. Johnston claims she is not shamed by her homosexuality. She also dares to tell men that she doesn't need their approval; that she has a sexuality and a personhood independent of male approval.

There is something in her critique of maleness that intrigues me, I who at a dinner party can feel like a dead person because someone says of some *other* woman, "Poor So-and-so, no man will have her." I am so dependent on men's opinions that I hate and fear them as the heroin addict hates and fears his pusher. I am taken by Jill's outspoken desire to define a woman's culture and to look closely at who women are and why they continue to judge themselves by standards set by men. It's finally my reporter's sense. This is the story. The social pariah, a gifted writer, who's shoving herself up the world's ass by saying, "I've got confidence. I'm not shamed. I'm lesbian. I make love to women. I neck with them in public. And I may be right. You are all repressed, uptight, and wrong. *All women are lesbians."* She fearlessly turns Freud on his Oedipal ear. Women love their mothers first, she explains, then they are forced by their mothers' powerlessness to transfer their infant-sexual love to their fathers, an unnatural act that lesbians don't make.

But I don't want to find out if I'm a lesbian. I don't want an involuntary twitch of feeling when a woman touches me. The idea of getting to know Jill scares me so much that I am convinced that I have to go through with it. It's a long way from my parents' small middle-class Philadelphia house

with its tiny green lawn and that one sycamore tree outside
the front window, but it's where I'm going to push myself now.
Counter-phobia. I guess I fear death more than anything. I
wonder if this means that someday I'll dare suicide?

I reread the folder of Johnston's *Newsweek* file and scan
the breathless manifesto she read at a debate chaired by Nor-
man Mailer, who'd tried to stop her speech before two of her
girl friends rushed the stage to neck with her.

"I am a woman-identified woman. I grew up in a society
of women—my mother and grandmother and then at an Episcopal boarding school. I dig women more than most women
do . . ."

December 4

When I talk to Jill Johnston by telephone, she sounds
frantic. Her voice is sweet and husky. We arrange to meet for
an introductory drink on Madison Avenue near *Newsweek's*
office. As I enter the dark bar, I see a tall figure with scraggly
long hair and a bulky dungaree jacket rise in one booth and
then sit down as though her joints had been too stiff to execute
the move. She tosses a few stringy bits of her hair nervously
over her shoulder and extends her hand with boarding school
courtesy. She is a confusing mixture of masculine and feminine style. Her voice is girlish and she speaks shyly in rushes
interspersed with high-pitched giggles. She avoids my eyes. I
realize that despite her bravado she is as scared of me as I am
of her. "Well, groovy. At least you're good-looking."

She pulls nervously on the lapels of her denim jacket,
and I try not to stare at the red stars and multicolored army
insignia embroidered onto it. She's wearing low-cut, tight
men's pants with a leather belt. Above the belt a loose-fitting
men's shirt does not hide the outline of breasts. As she stands

to get another drink, I see her cartoony-huge masculine lace-up mountain boots. She carries an army khaki pack with a mermaid sewed onto it as a handbag, and between her breasts flops a hanging collage of found objects (a third breast, she once wrote), including a lanyard made for her by her fourteen-year-old son Richard, several keys to now-abandoned cars, and a medal of the madonna and child.

I like the fact that she walks with a long, athletic lope, the way I used to as a teen-ager. Her body is strong. She has tiny childish teeth and a boisterous laugh, but the lines in her freckled face below pale eyebrows and green eyes filled with child cunning make her look like a ravaged adolescent. As she moves the clangs of her necklace reinforce my impression that she's a sweet Frankenstein monster. Like a scarecrow, she is made up of a series of unmatching parts and looks freaky, funky, and huggable.

I am awed by my bravery as I stare at her across the booth. I've kept the appointment.

After a minute or so of chatter, I am falling under her spell. She talks directly to me, sensing my shyness, first finding out that I am newly separated from my husband, in pain, and trying to write at *Newsweek*. She tells me she's a woman-identified woman—a lesbian feminist. She tells me she's into serial monogamy, meaning one single lover at a time. I am very impressed to hear her define her state of mind and being so succinctly. She prattles on: "The old butch-femme distinction, stereotyped passive or aggressive homosexual, is ridiculous. Like most lesbians I'm happily confused. I'm intellectually aggressive and aggressive as an athlete and a dancer, but sexually most women are passive. I guess when I find somebody I really like I become more aggressive."

My mind is measuring and trying to memorize her words as she speaks. So many questions. Are most women passive? Serial monogamy, does it hurt less, is it a better kind of expectation for all of us? Maybe it's the wave of the future. The man or woman gets down on one knee and says, "Marry me, darling. We'll draw up a contract from the church of your choice binding us for the next four and a half years."

But I wonder if Jill is the sort of woman who makes men joke about feminism saying, "You're all dykes anyhow." Is there some place where I can identify with a woman who wants to love only women? She ends her conversation by peering at me and demanding, "How can you work at that Middle-American white male power club *Newsweek?* Wouldn't you like to write about things from your point of view, instead of adding ten years and a penis to your perspective?"

I listen to her speak and I waver between dismissing her as a crank and drinking in her words like a thirsty traveler. She continues, "I don't think they'd like you. You probably arouse a threatened attitude in the men with your cool intellectuality."

Seduction, mental, a familiar tactic employed by the subjects of my articles, but never done so well. My mind is relaxed, open—I feel bewitched. But then my nerves jump as she opens the fabled notebook from which she writes her weekly *Village Voice* column and reads me the latest line, "I want to be fucked by a woman and walk like an ostrich from cosmic and cataclysmic orgasms."

I knock over my glass as I reach for my cigarettes. She watches me recover the glass and shouts with laughter. "You're not as uptight as you think you are. I like you. Let's get out of here." She strides out, walking with that swagger I've never seen on an adult woman. I wave to the waiter and pay the check. She's consumed several Bloody Marys. I pay for them and my Coke.

Bits of her conversation stick in my mind. She is an intellectual with a nearly crank intelligence, poring over books and from them deducing a justification for her life. "Indigenous modern dance is matriarchal, you know," she says, as I lengthen my stride to keep up with her in the street. I shake my head, no, I don't know, determined not to fake knowledge. "Isadora is the best known. Then there's Ruth St. Denis. They come from the tradition of women as exhibitionist sex objects. It goes back to the days of the temple prostitutes."

December 22

Two nights ago, I went to a lesbian dance with Jill Johnston. I had been apprehensively silent as Jill parked her van on a deserted street in the Bowery, dark except for a red glow behind a fire escape where a few people sat. "Are they men or women?" Jill asked, and then giggled as she slammed the car door closed.

Rock music blared from the red-lit windows. We walked up a dark broken staircase past a hand-painted sign on the wall "Daughters of Bilitis." Inside the loft room felt seedy. A few bridge chairs, frantic red strobe lights, and a giant Janis Joplin poster were the only furnishings. The thirty women looked dispirited and bored. They were of all ages—fat-thin, ugly-pretty—and didn't look different from the women you'd see on a Village street corner. In fact, the afternoon after the dance, everytime I'd see two women walking together in the street, I would stare and then picture them necking. When I first walked into the dance I kept trying to figure out what my reaction was. Suddenly my throat started to hurt. I had no expectations about what a lesbian dance would be like. One woman with a kind smile, long curly hair, and a lot of rings on, noticed me writing in my notebook and asked if I was gay or straight. When I said I was straight, she said wistfully, "You're lucky. Too bad for me though."

When two slightly overweight women in new-looking dungarees finally stood up to dance, they moved slowly despite the fast music, their cheeks touching, their arms around each other's necks 1950s-style. Every once in a while they'd kiss passionately. One skinny woman in a man's sailor suit and hat was gyrating by herself. Two other women were bear-hugging, their bodies swaying, their feet stationary. One of them was wearing a pair of denim farm overalls, and her large breasts were hanging out bare on either side of the bib; the other woman's red cardigan was unbuttoned, exposing her breasts. I shivered. Were these women doing something I would love to do if I weren't so uptight? Was this a scene from my nightmares or my fantasies?

Sometimes the thirty women fox-trotting under the strobe lights looked to me like the teen-age girls dancing together at lunch period at my junior high school. The older women looked like people you'd see at a Marxist meeting, except for the dancing and the self-conscious necking. But then again their open-mouthed kissing didn't seem very real, it seemed kind of stagey, in the service of ideology. After a while the scene began to look like a pornographic cliché, and I remembered cheesecake pictures of Danish sex kittens in magazines for men. I suddenly thought that some of my male friends might envy my witnessing the scene. And I felt protective toward the women, knowing I might be writing about them for a male audience.

When the music stopped, Jill wandered over to me. The girl with the large bare breasts followed her. I strolled out of earshot, and noticed that they were beginning an animated conversation. Suddenly, Jill started to laugh and began to dance with the girl whose breasts were now bobbing again. Then they were hugging very tight, and Jill kissed her lips gently, holding her face between her hands. They hugged again and Jill rolled her hips and her crotch against the girl.

I stood there in the darkness, hoping that at least I was invisible with all the queasiness I was feeling, and then a young blond girl with an angel face and narrow hips came over to ask me to dance. "No, ahh, I have a sore throat," I said, touching her arm apologetically. I was sipping my third glass of warm white wine. Her lips tightened like mine might if I got up my nerve to ask some guy to dance and he said no. Then she nodded, looked down, and walked away to stand on the other side of the room.

Jill was stroking the shoulders of a young girl with green eyes and long black hair. The girl stared into Jill's eyes, ran her hand down Jill's arm, and reached into Jill's dungaree jacket pocket to pull out a purple pen. She broke eye contact to pick up Jill's hand and draw a double-female lesbian sign on her palm. "You're branded for life," the girl said intensely. Jill laughed. "Let's dance," she said and put both hands around the girl's waist, pulling her close. "I can't," said the girl, caressing Jill's back.

So Jill started dancing by herself, first a solemn ballerina-twirl, then a hammy clown pirouette, and finally an athletic twist. She danced over to me standing in the dark, and held open her arms while swaying slowly, a hypnotically seductive gesture. She grabbed me and hugged me. I felt her soft, maternal breasts. I had been watching her now for several weeks hugging, touching, and flirting with women. To accommodate the strangeness, I guess, I had started to believe she was a man. But breasts. How could a woman act like that? How could a woman touch another woman's breasts? But worse than that, I had that funny sexy feeling tingling along my skin on my stomach. Then the shame overwhelmed me. All the worthless feelings I've ever felt about myself flooded back in a giant lump. What would my mother say? How my ex-husband would nod and laugh harshly at the news. My legs felt weak. I nodded to Jill apologetically. "Jill, it would ruin the objectivity of my article if I danced with you," I said, quickly holding her arm to reassure her as she pulled away. "Aw, shit," she laughed, relieved, I think, for an ex-

cuse to avoid our encounter. She danced away and was soon
throwing her arms and legs around in a wild dance with the
woman in the unbuttoned red cardigan.

I looked around, sighing. The women were looking less
and less real dancing under the red strobes. I don't understand how people can meet for the first time and immediately
start openly and passionately necking. It doesn't happen at
heterosexual dances. Several of the women sitting on bridge
chairs were now drinking beer from cans. Four women linked
arms and began a cakewalk across the floor, singing along to
the record. "It's too late baby naow. There's something inside,
I feel I can't make it, ohoo, *no-aa-oo*."

While they sang, my mood improved. I began to feel silly
for having been so afraid. Nothing bad could happen to me
here. I watched my blond-haired friend looking at her beer
can and leaning against a far wall by herself. I walked over to
her, and touched her on the shoulder. We began to dance the
twist, I felt strained, but determined to keep going. When Jill
saw me dancing she threw her head back and kicked her left
leg up in the air, and then she doubled over with glee. She
twisted over to us and we all danced to the end of the record of
Janis Joplin singing "Bobby McGee," each of us doing a
private, dutiful twist. My mind was split into three parts as
usual when I'm on assignment. I was dancing with the blond
woman and with Jill because it would be a great thing to
describe in the piece, right? Or was I dancing with them because I wanted to? But this is one reason why I am a reporter.
I can assume a fearless, or less fearful persona to explore the
world. Jill hit me affectionately on the shoulder when the
dance was over, and I felt as though I'd come through a major
psychic journey. I'd felt physical attraction for a woman. I'd
watched women hugging and kissing each other. And I haven't
gone mad or felt less myself.

JANUARY

January 23

Sometimes I feel the parts of my life don't organize into a whole person. I am a different me, depending on who I'm with. That's how I know I haven't got things figured out yet. Jill Johnston has become an exhausting fixture in my life. On Saturday mornings she parks her van downstairs, thunders up the twelve flights in step-skipping leaps (she has elevator phobia), and pounds my door. Once inside she questions me intensely, "Are any rapists around?" and she'll run from the living room as if to rout any men out. I know from interviewing her old friends that she often forms relationships of extreme possessiveness.

I guess I enjoy her fixation on me. She is the first woman I've spent this much time observing for an article and the first person who has insisted I am an equal. I wind up telling her things about myself that I haven't figured out before: I never get sexually turned on to anybody who isn't turned on to me, perhaps because it's safe, and I'm fearful. The intimacy she demands is flattering. Since I am her biographer, of sorts, I am becoming the person, besides her lover, in whom

212   *Susan Braudy*

she has confided and invested the most. For this reason, I know, I am important to her.

"Where are they? Where are they?" she mutters as the doorbell clangs. "Usually there are so many men here I could be raped." "Oh Jill, don't flatter yourself," says her girl friend in the doorway. Her heavy hiking boots thundering over my bare wood floors, Jill raises her eyebrows haughtily and then smiles. "I like the way you're changing the furniture in this place. It's inviting. You've added color, the red rug and all. Now I can sit in the living room and feel good." She pounds me on the back. "You're less depressed and more into discovering you than you were two months ago." I glow.

But she's not always sweet. At the end of an evening's drinking at some funky-chic Village bar, she'll gallantly try to cruise the waitress and then, as if answering my uneasy shifting in my seat over the spectacle, she'll pound the table and scream, "Straight women. I hate you all."

Yesterday her visit went badly. I was lying half-awake in bed at 9:00 A.M. when I heard her familiar clomping and then pounding on my bedroom door. She'd come right in through the front door without ringing the bell. My old college friend Fred had said he might be coming in late to sleep over, since his apartment was being painted. So I'd tucked sheets over the living room couch and unlocked the door.

When I heard her saying my name outside the bedroom door, my irritation nearly choked me. First, why didn't she call me before she came? New Yorkers never visit each other unannounced. Second, I was not sleeping alone. James and I had finally gone to sleep at 3:00 A.M. after a television movie. If Jill burst into my bedroom while a young man was sleeping there, nobody would come out unbloodied. And the prospect of an uninvited, disapproving third person made me angry. "Jill," I yelled, spacing my words distinctly. "Go away, I'm sleeping. I don't want to be bothered. I'm sleeping. Go away."

"You fucking bitch. You straight woman," she sobbed,

but she didn't open the door, thank God, and fast clomps indicated she was running back into the living room. I cursed silently watching James's frightened face. "Is she gone?" He looked a little silly pulling the sheet up over his chin. "I'm getting out of here."

"Wait," I sighed a huge sigh of duty. "I'll get up to see her. You get dressed and sneak into the dining room, pretending you came in from the outside." We were both scared of the scene that Jill could make. I also felt a little self-important to be the object of such passion. It was on the verge of an adventure if I could handle all the elements without any disastrous confrontation. James sat up on the side of the bed. "Hurry up," I said. "She likes to come in here." His shoulders made a silent leap of fear and he began to hunt for his clothes.

As I tied my bathrobe, I pondered my cowardice. Jill necks with her girl friends in front of me constantly. Now when she tried to invade my bedroom, I felt apologetic. I couldn't reveal my private life, for fear she'd make an ugly scene, hurt James's feelings or feel betrayed herself.

Out in my living room, I peered frantically into corners. She had disappeared. On impulse, I opened the service door leading to the stairs. Sure enough, Jill was lying on her back on my two trash cans, tears all over her face. Her head was leaning against the wall. I was impressed by the dramatic impact of her stance. Loud sobs filled the metal hallway with echoes. "Bitch, bitch. Why do I get friendly with straight bitches? Don't I have enough trouble?"

Despite my reluctant aesthetic appreciation of her scene, my stomach hurt from watching her cry. "Come in. I'll make you a cup of tea," I said formally, but my voice was shaky. She snuffled loudly with reproach, wiping her eyes and nose on her coat sleeves. She watched me balefully out of bloodshot green eyes as she pulled herself off the teetering trash cans. I filled the teapot with water and excused myself, leaving her sitting at the kitchen table, her tears forgotten, her head bent over a copy of the *Village Voice*. In my room, James was fumbling with the gold buttons on his navy blazer. "Hurry up." I was impatient with his confusion. He shook his hair out of his eyes. "What should I do?" "Go out the living room door and ring the bell." I was stumbling around the bed, knocking my shins on the hardwood corners of the bed's frame in an effort to make it look tidy, as though no one had been sleeping in it. I didn't look as he walked out. A few seconds later Jill poked her head inside the door. "Lookit, why are you hiding? I gotta talk to you."

I was amazed that she had not crossed paths with James in the hallway. A second later the doorbell rang, and I let James in. "Oh Jesus Christ, a boy, it's a nightmare around here," I heard Jill mumbling behind me.

I followed her into the kitchen and he followed me. He couldn't stop staring at her and stood formally by a chair waiting for her to sit down first. I was hoping that she would at least like him for his patrician good looks. She's a terrific Anglophile and snob. She snorted somewhat shyly while I introduced them, and then flopped into a chair. She leaned back precariously and boldly on its base, and talked to me as though he wasn't there. Relieved to escape scrutiny, he sat down to stare at her as though she was a creature from another solar system, every aspect of whose physiognomy he must commit to memory.

"I hear they're not using your article about me," she said, fixing a glare at me. "How you ever expected those uptight establishment pigs at *Esquire* to accept an article about a dirty dyke written by a feminist is beyond me. And why you won't let me look at it and see if I can fix it up, kills me too." "Jill," I said, "how could that be? They've told me all along that they are going to use the piece." She'd brought up two sore points. First, I can usually reassure Jill when she worries about friends turning off her or about unsympathetic editors. But the thought of my article being rejected upset me, too. Second, we've had a major battle of wills about her reading the piece. I never let people read what I write about them. I didn't want to think of her approval as I wrote it. Whenever she'd try to wheedle a look at it, I'd tell her it was a matter of my professionalism, and that usually shut her up.

"How do you know my piece was rejected?" I asked her. "Oh, some girl who works in the editorial department came to Bonnie and Clyde's bar last night and she told me it was being bumped from the women's issue." I was down. It doesn't take much these days to knock me off my precarious perch. I'd spent all that time following Jill around, memorizing her every move, taping her answers to my questions, hanging around gay bars, going for weekends to her country house, and for what—to lose an assignment? "Maybe she's wrong," I answered, knowing that she was not wrong, that the reason I hadn't been able to get my editor on the telephone for the last two weeks had been made suddenly clear.

Having succeeded in upsetting me, Jill turned a green eye on James. "What's your thing?" she asked with a provocative giggle. He shifted uncomfortably in his chair. "Well, Ma'am," he started, uncertain about whether he should even look at her, "right now I'm taking photographs."

"Ma'am," she giggled again and tilted her chair back against the refrigerator. "Ma'am. Nobody's called me Ma'am for years." Now she waggled a thumb in his direction. "What's with him anyway?" she said, winking at me.

I was angry. "Look, Jill, don't be nasty to him. He's not being nasty to you." I was struggling for control.

"Oh, bullshit." She jumped to her feet, pushing her half-filled teacup off the table. James obediently reached down to pick it up off the floor. "Bullshit, I don't have to sit here at a table with this beautiful baby boy that you keep here to fuck. And I don't have to listen to your discussions of what I can and can't say. I'm getting out of here."

By the end of her tirade she was crying again. James was

tossing his hair out of his eyes with self-conscious desperation. I was tired. She was in pain but I should be getting some sympathy, too. No article. It's at times like this that I usually think of my ex-husband. I bet he doesn't have to get his Saturday mornings disrupted with messages of professional defeats. Ah, then I got the next depressed thought—maybe I'm not making it so well on my own after all. Jill was halfway out the front door, still throwing insults over her shoulder. "Remind me not to call you all the time and come pick you up and take you out to dinner anymore. Remind me to stick to my own kind. You're no feminist. Men in the morning. Men all over the house."

Then she was gone, and I turned to apologize to James, my hand on his shoulder. But he was grinning. "Gee, she sure is weird," he told me, "and not very attractive either." I started laughing, but not with a great deal of pleasure. "Not very pretty," I mimicked him the way she had been doing a few seconds before. "Jesus, James, you are a walking stereotype. You look at a lesbian and you decide to figure out if you want to sleep with her." "I don't want to sleep with her," he said, glaring at me. "But I bet it would probably cure her." I was silent. "Cure her." How could I explain to him that the cliché male reaction to lesbians is to brag you could convert them by giving them good sex. How do I start? It would take hours for me to cite evidence, draw on remarks he's made, and get through his defensiveness about his lack of experience.

So I stay silent and watch him drink his tea and shake his head and recompose the corners of his mouth and try not to giggle as he recalls the spectacle Jill has made. I felt lonely. If he and Jill are like two beings with a different language and different brain, I am someplace else—able to get along with both of them, but feeling that I am not and cannot be what either of them wants me to be.

January 30

People say they feel pathetic eating a solitary late-night hamburger, but right now I love it. When I was growing up, my mother ruled restaurant food nutritionally worthless. Consequently we almost never ate out. My big adventure was to leave the watery egg, vitamin pills, and oatmeal breakfast untouched, and then to order a morning hamburger at the greasy spoon near my high school.

Once we were married, Paul believed in home eating. So if I got home late *hoping* we'd go for dinner at a Chinese or Japanese restaurant, he'd usually be whistling in the kitchen, his cauliflower soup steaming.

But now I have no mealtime responsibilities. At the luncheonette counter last night near *Newsweek* I pulled the roll off my cheeseburger and shot the ketchup lovingly into the cheese.

"That looks awful," said one of *Newsweek's* senior editors, sitting down hard on the counter stool next to mine. I have noticed that he and I and Lynn, who is the other woman writer, are the three late-night *Newsweek* workers. Maybe sometime I'll be a big-time editor like him. I work as many hours a day as he does.

He lives in his office where a pile of soiled shirts fills a corner. One night we met at the water cooler on the corridor between our two offices and he questioned me closely about why I'd stopped free-lancing and come to *Newsweek*. I told him I'd needed the discipline of a desk job since my marriage had broken up. "Me, too," he had said unexpectedly. "When I broke up my marriage, I threw myself into a job here. It saved my life. I needed the structure."

At the luncheonette counter, he again surprised me with his candor. "I'm in a quandary. *Newsweek* lawyers tell me I've got to hire a woman writer in my department. Otherwise your women's group will get me for discrimination."

"That looks good," he said gesturing with his thumb at my cheeseburger. "I'll have the same."

"Wait a minute," and he leaned away from me, raising his hands as though he'd just discovered I was sitting next to him. "You're a *Newsweek* writer and a woman, right? You should come into my department."

His invitation was a compliment to my *Newsweek* success, though it probably had more to do with his legal jam. And it was true that I'd suggested several good story ideas for his department during our water-cooler chats.

"I'll see," I said, knowing I would eventually turn down the offer. "I mean, I'd feel I was deserting my editor. He's spending a lot of time training me." He shrugged. "All I'm saying is think about it."

FEBRUARY

February 3

Alice told me she keeps a diary that has become volumes of her complaints. She says it doesn't occur to her to write about happy moments. Many women write diaries. It's amazing to think of the thousands of secret pages about the inner lives of women. For me, this diary is my way of confronting sad moods. Writing unhappy thoughts down, and then reading my words a few days later is therapeutic. I learn that self-pity and deep depression are impermanent.

Like Alice, I rarely use these pages to write about happy situations. I've decided to do that tonight. I have written almost nothing about Fred, though I've even shown him entries from this diary. We've never slept together and there's something so sane and loving about the way we treat each other. I wish I could feel so easy about a man I was sleeping with. I wish I could ignore a stupid anecdote he might tell at a party or not feel threatened by losing his approval. I wish I could just let him be.

Several nights a week Fred comes to my office and swivels back and forth in Jim's desk chair and reads while I write. He

teaches philosophy and is curious about *Newsweek* people and
its corporate atmosphere, since it is so different from his world.
After work tonight we went to the luncheonette for a sandwich. I found myself interviewing him about how men feel
about women and sex. If Paul had confessed he was always
turned on by blondes who made passes at him, or by women
wearing turbans like his mother's, I'd have been jealous. So I
never asked him about such things. But I'm not upset with
Fred's answers, so I'm free to question. When I was married
I felt disloyal to Paul if I talked about sex with other men.
Now I crave information.

"Suppose a woman says she wants to have sex with you,"
I began tonight as I gulped down a tuna sandwich. He paused.
"Look, it's flattering, even if she's not my type." Fred is logi-
cal. He refined my question. "What you're asking is, how successful is a pass made by a woman. Frankly, unless a guy's a
movie star and bored by it, a woman's got it made. She'll
score the guy for one night anyway."

I pondered his answer. Then I explained, "Women say
men are lucky because they can pick and choose. They don't
have to wait for the telephone to ring." "Yeah," he interrupted,
"but men feel shitty if they're rejected. Who likes to be rejected?" He twisted his full mouth into an ironic smile. I smiled
back at him, noting that he looked slightly out of place in this
slick Madison Avenue deli, with his worn tweed coat left over
from graduate school, his beard, and his rumpled workshirt.

We have known each other since high school, but I have
never talked to him as I do now. Part of getting married,
Paul once told me, is to give up other deep friendships. For
me, a way of getting over the loss of a husband/best friend is
making new bonds with new people, though sometimes after
I wave good-night to Fred from my cab, I feel lonely.

"My house is a mess," I told him at the luncheonette,
changing the subject. "I spend most nights at *Newsweek*. The
books and records Paul left behind are falling off the shelves.

I haven't paid any bills this month. It makes me crazy to think about them."

"I have no plans for tonight," he answered. "Why don't we do it together? I've been paying my bills for ten years. I could give you a few tips."

So we paid our check and I hailed the black limousine parked on Madison Avenue that the magazine hires to take home late-night toilers. I get a kick out of the fact that Fred likes to ride in the slick, silent machine.

At my house, he started piling my phonograph records in alphabetical order. Paul took only a few records because I'd been so nasty about the books he'd piled into carton after carton.

I wonder why dividing books and records has caused me such pain. In one of our early telephone conversations I'd sputtered, "Take any goddam furniture you want, Paul. The loot is not books or chairs. I'm going to fight you to the end for our friends. I'm not giving up one of them." But I guess I wasn't admitting the whole truth. I made him take the original editions of his books on Cromwell. I had urged him to buy them one summer while we were in England. But even though they are valuable they aren't mine, and I don't miss them. But the posters and the table and the ordinary books he took feel like assaults on me.

As we work I am impressed by Fred's precise habits. He answers my questions about my checkbook, and I watch him, thinking that he reads four books a week, eats cottage cheese or eggs for breakfast, vacuums his floors, and sees movies by directors he admires. He also runs a mile and writes his philosophy essays daily. He doesn't feel the panic that is part of every one of my days. He knows who he is, so thoughts about his future don't terrorize him.

I am discovering that he is interested in people as well as books. So he and I spend hours in restaurants talking about whether we know a happy marriage, or why either of us would get married. We take turns citing our own lives as evidence. "Remember that girl I went out with sophomore year of college?" he asked. "Yeah, the Black girl you took to the Pete Seeger concert," I might answer, dying to hear what he's going to say about her after all these years. "Well, we were in love. But I remember when you and Paul decided to get married, we couldn't understand why you did it. We felt like kids. And you know, I still feel marriage is something older people do."

February 20

I typed tonight, sitting on my leg, the other knee against my desk. I have back trouble. Over the past three weeks, I've spent hours squirming to find a position that doesn't hurt my lower back.

Yesterday the orthopedist turned me one way and then the other way on a table to take pictures of my spine, lovely pictures of a ghostly chain, and sighed as he said that I was too young to have a muscular weakness in my back. He prescribed a steel-ribbed corset that I am picking up tomorrow. When I told my shrink that a lifetime of back trouble depressed me, she answered, shortly, "Some people somatize. Others have nervous breakdowns."

I was irritated, so she explained the new word "somatize" in a kinder tone. "Instead of feeling deeply upset about your marriage breakup and your new *Newsweek* job, you've translated your anxiety into a physical ailment."

Newsweek does present problems. It took them three months of trying me out at half-salary to decide they wanted to hire me. Originally I'd been promised a tryout of one month only. And I was hired on full salary only after I had summoned my nerve to ask my editor about the delay. I notice that if you act important here, you get treated better. A lot of the male writers here have had far less experience than I, but they speak with authority in situations where I remain shyly silent.

But I am determined to learn *Newsweek's* writing style. Everyone jokes about how I stay here into the night writing, rewriting, studying *Newsweek* articles. In each issue I underline the best topic sentences and adverbial hooks at the beginnings of sentences. I also read *Rolling Stone, Variety, Columbia Journalism Review,* and the women's magazines searching for story ideas.

I am making a few friends. One of them is Lynn Young, the other female writer. Everyone is always comparing our work, as though we're two horses running a private race. One man literally walked backward out of my office when I asked him to stop comparing my writing to Lynn's. "Getting a little doctrinaire women's lib, aren't you?" he said.

MARCH

March 2

Last night after the cleaning woman emptied my wastebasket and dusted slowly around me and the mess of papers on my desk, Lynn walked past my office. She leaned her head against the wall as we started a halting conversation. As we spoke, she rubbed her eyebrows with her fingers in a gesture of weariness. With her year-round tan, her face manages to look both Jewish and Polynesian. She stands like a ballerina, her ribcage high, shoulders back. She wears tight polo shirts and pants, and seems not to care about how she looks. Her fingernails are bitten.

After a few questions about her story this week, I began to quiz her about her *Newsweek* career. She told me how our editor had refused at first to give her writing assignments week after week, even after she'd been promoted from researcher to writer. Other people had told me she'd been one of the leaders of the women's insurrection, had negotiated a legal suit, and finally forced management to agree to hire women writers, and eventually senior editors. She then or-

ganized a writing class to encourage intimidated female researchers to write under less stress than the tryout.

I told her, "If I'd have come to *Newsweek* from college,
I never would've had the guts to take a writing tryout. After
you've been here for three years, even if you were Mary Mc-
Carthy, you'd believe what they believe—that women can't
write under pressure the way men can."

"It's bullshit," she responded and ran her fingers across
her forehead again. "But it took me months to turn them
around myself. They hoped I'd go away quietly."

"But it's not going to be that hard for you, you're lucky,"
she said. I hear a tinge of envy in her voice, though her words
are kind. "Our editor likes you. He'll train you to write *Newsweek* style. It's not something you're born with. Somebody
has taken the time to train every good male *Newsweek* writer."

She was looking at me with concern. "Why are you sitting
like that?" I explained to her that my back has gone out and
that I'm wearing a steel-ribbed corset. "Somatizing," she was
still looking at me with maternal affection. "God, I know
this place is hard on people. You're married, aren't you?"

I looked away for a second and then began to outline
to her the details of my separation. She started to twirl a
piece of her hair. "These things are hard." She was shaking
her head. "Do you have anybody else?" "No, but I have lots
of friends," I answered her, with a rush of self-pity based in
part on the anxious look around her eyes. I also realized that
I was defining something I hadn't said before. I am not in
love with anyone. "Well, if you need any help with your work
or just want to talk, let's get together," she said, smiling and
pushing herself away from the wall she was leaning on. "What
about a cup of coffee at about ten?" I asked, afraid to show
how much I wanted to keep talking to her. She pulled her
striped polo shirt sleeve off her wrist to check her watch.
"Okay, I just have to send out a few cable queries and clear
my desk. Come by for me."

March 30

I have been re-adding the figures in my bank and check-ing accounts. I am obsessed with the idea that I won't have enough money to live on if I keep buying so much clothing. I am also worried about my job. Before I came to *Newsweek*, I never understood the fear and energy people put into office politics.

At previous jobs in New Haven I always felt superior to the buzz that followed a memo announcing somebody's promotion to junior vice-president of public relations.

Now everybody in my department is plunged into talk and turmoil. We are getting a new editor. This morning Lynn waved her paper coffee cup at me, beckoning me into her office. She couldn't talk because she was cradling a telephone on her shoulder and talking to the Florida bureau, while she was licking crumbs of her cheese danish off her fingers. After she hung up, she announced, "We are getting a new editor. It seems Walter is leaving to write a book. Some say he's being axed."

I was stunned. I had conceived of my job here partly as an alliance between me and my editor. After all, he'd recruited me and was, as Lynn said, giving me special training: the first training a woman writer had received. I'd even turned down the offer to go write for the other senior editor I met at the luncheonette because I felt loyalty to my editor. Now this.

"I wouldn't worry yet," Lynn advised. I was learning about her analytic skills. She knew everything that happened at *Newsweek*. Through the women's action that she'd led, she made friends with secretaries, researchers, and reception-ists throughout the *Newsweek* empire.

She explained: "Tomorrow, everybody in the department will get a memo. Alice Jones upstairs typed it up an hour ago." My back started to ache. I stared at Lynn while she shoved papers into a bottom drawer of her desk. "What does it mean for us?" I finally asked. "Well, nothing is going to change right away," she said. "For me, it's an improvement. Walter has never wanted me around," Lynn said, raising her blue eyes to look at me. She was choosing her words carefully. "But for you, well, Walter really likes you. He hired you and he's brought you along. Another editor may not be as partial toward you."

I knew she was warning me.

APRIL

April 10

My new editor has been meeting each of his writers this morning. I entered his office and I noticed that my former editor's office decorations were piled on the floor—a photograph of a family of nudes was on its side. On his huge desk were two new additions, pictures in gold frames of a woman and two children—the tokens of corporate wars. My new editor is a heavy man with white, white skin, not much older than I am, but with his voluminous dark suits, short hair, and heavy, black-framed glasses, he could be ten years older. In *Newsweek* terms, he is two generations ahead of me, having written crash cover stories on the Vietnam war in one-night stands, the stuff of *Newsweek* legends.

He tapped the eraser end of his pencil on his desk over and over as he spoke. "Well, I hope we'll work well together. You are coming along, Susan, aren't you?" His voice was a formal singsong, and I noticed that he put my name familiarly, in the middle of every other sentence, a trick someone once told me you learn at Dale Carnegie. "You are, of course, a good writer. The question, Susan, is how good a *Newsweek* writer you are going to become. And I'm here to promise to help you."

He stood formally jiggling the change in his pocket and signifying our interview was over. He'd pulled the rug out under me. I am a *Newsweek* writer I tell myself. My stories go into the magazine. Sure, they are edited, but that's the game here. My name is on the masthead as an associate editor: but this man made it clear that he thinks I am still on tryout.

I can't stop thinking about what would happen if I lost my job. It makes my stomach hurt. I keep jotting down figures. I should save $150 a week from now on. Tomorrow I'll call the payroll office and ask to have money transferred to my savings account from my paycheck every Monday. In the old days Paul was constantly recalculating our finances in order to prove that I was spending too much money. He irritated me, but I see now that his fears freed *me* from the need to worry.

MAY

May 2

It's happening. I feel my editor's disapproval. And I am fighting back, without a Paul to get angry on my behalf and bolster my ego. I keep wondering if I should have thanked my editor that day he told me he was going to help me along. Soon after the first talk he summoned me again and told me that I would no longer write feature stories. Instead I would be doing intricate one-paragraph news items on such subjects as the latest Federal Communications Commission rulings. I blurted out, "But Walter hired me as a feature writer. I mean I have no experience writing hard news."

He spoke quickly. "Walter doesn't work here anymore. And I'm trying, Susan, to correct errors he made. You're a new writer. You shouldn't write the choice assignments, week after week, if you follow me. You'll learn to write short articles."

His words make me work even later on Friday nights rewriting the tiny pieces. For a break I do sums about what I'd need to earn if I started free-lancing again. I keep wondering if I'm overreacting. I asked Lynn and she sighed. "Well, yes and no. Let's put it this way. He's not helping you, right?"

It's true. With Walter, before I started to write, he'd ask me about the organization of my piece. Then he'd correct me where he thought I was wrong. And often he asked me to stand behind his left shoulder while he pencil-edited my article, explaining his corrections. Now the new editor gives me my weekly assignment in two sentences. If I ask him about it, he waves me away with a half-laugh, explaining that he's under deadline pressure. When I turn in my final copy, he rewrites most of it, typing between the lines I've written: a public humiliation here.

It's awful. I mope around the house weekends, trying to figure out what to do. Paul has called a few times to ask me for lunch. I've claimed I was too busy. I don't want him to see me down or defeated. Lynn advises, "Read *Newsweek* stories. Analyze the leads. There are four leads, Susan. First there's the general-truth lead that pertains to your story. There's also the list of surprising new things that are a result of your story. Another lead is the who, what, why. Then there's the newspaper lead. And don't forget the joke."

Yesterday I got tranquilizers, so I won't sap my strength staying up nights and worrying.

May 20

Today I ran out into the corridor to catch a word with the senior editor who tried to hire me for his department that night in the luncheonette. My back is still out, but I can hardly feel my corset, except that it sticks into me every time I stand or bend at the waist. "I want to talk to you a second," I said, touching his shoulder. His lips pursed, he stroked his beard with a thumb. "Remember our conversation the other week?" I continued quickly. "Well, I'd love to come to work for you now."

"Dear heart, I have already filled the place in my department." I heard indifference in his final words. "Dear heart,
early birds get the worms."

May 28

At dinner, Lynn asked me whether I was divorced yet.
I am behaving like an ostrich, but I haven't even marked the
upcoming court date on my calendar. I pushed Paul to do
the suing, partly because he seemed reluctant. He doesn't
seem to want a divorce. I assume he likes to feel "bohemianly"
in transition, rather than divorced and available. Do I want
a divorce? I don't know, but I forced it because I'll do anything to unsettle him. We're still fighting. I don't think about
the date. I don't want to focus on such a painful anniversary.
I'd rather feel the pain now and then in little bits.

I tell myself that deciding to divorce is as good as doing
it. Who the hell needs legal papers and ceremonies? I read
about a New Jersey minister who has invented a divorce
ceremony. He believes a couple should stand before their
peers in a ceremonial posture—under the aegis of the church
—and publicly dissolve the marriage. I had trouble standing
up to proclaim my marriage to my relatives and friends. I
won't be ceremonial about its failure. I feel furtive, shamed,
and private.

JUNE

June 5

Last night I was at work until midnight. I spent five hours rewriting my paragraph on the legal ins and outs of de-sexgregating Mory's, the Yale eating club. By 11:00 P.M. I had a paragraph of six convoluted sentences. I am caught. No matter what I decide to write, my editor will rewrite it. If I write "35%" he runs a dark line through my words and prints "thirty-five percent." If in the next story I write out a number in words, he makes it a numeral again. When I ask him why, he looks down at his desk, and says, "It's not something I can explain, Susan."

I keep quizzing Lynn. Why is he editing me so heavily? Am I about to be fired? Yesterday, she answered, "Well, it doesn't mean anything good. You probably won't be fired because of the women's suit. But you're not being encouraged." "Should I be looking for another job?" I asked her falteringly. "Another job." Her fingers were pressing against her mouth. "Yes."

So I did it. I dialed information for the office number of *Ms.* magazine. And I made an appointment to see Gloria Steinem today. Ever since I read the first issue of the new magazine I'd been dying to write for it. But I've been telling myself Gloria knows who and where I am. If she had any need for me, she'd call me.

However, this afternoon, I rushed downstairs and hailed a cab to another anonymous looking skyscraper.

The *Ms.* office is one big desk littered with envelopes, and two tiny rooms to the side. Gloria sat in one room talking on the phone. I realized she looked incongruous because she had told me that she'd never had a desk job; that, like her father, she had always worked alone, at her own pace.

So I sat in the reception area listening to the telephones ring, listening to Gloria's classy Midwestern voice talk comfortingly on the phone to a woman who, I began to understand, had been in jail for a few days in Texas after she was arrested on an angry union picket line. When Gloria hung up she took my shoulders and kissed me on the cheek, but she seemed preoccupied.

"Well, what's new?" she asked when we settled back at her tiny desk. I got to the point. "I'm not happy with *Newsweek,* and they're not happy with me."

She folded her hands and began to tell me about the various places she'd been fired from. A publisher at *Seventeen* magazine had thought she was a pinko because she supported Angela Davis, and fired her as contributing editor. A worried glance at me, and she began to list editors I should ask for free-lance assignments. Finally she stopped and I asked, "Well, what about here? I mean, I'd love to come here."

"We have a lot of editors who worked for very little on the sample issue who have to be hired first. Besides, you should be doing your own work: you want to write, not edit. You should be writing for us," she answered me, leaning forward and touching my knee sympathetically. So I kissed her goodbye, nearly missing her cheek with awkwardness, and left the office. I felt I'd been turned down. Of course I wasn't in any worse shape for asking. But I have no fantasy of escape.

And by the time I got back to *Newsweek,* my depression had solidified like a huge cocoon made out of steel wool.

June 10

Two days ago, I got a book to review from the *Village Voice.* I'd never even met the editor who sent it to me. It's called *They Got What They Wanted,* a novel by Phyllis Raphael about a woman's exit from her marriage. I feel like the author bored a little hole in my head and pulled out some of my brain. So at six this morning, the first paragraph of my review sprung sentence after sentence in my head: "When I was younger, I believed adults were in charge of their emotional fates, holding their pens firmly as they wrote their own life stories. After my six-year marriage broke up about a year ago, I realized I knew as little about why people make decisions to get married and unmarried as I do about what is going on in my kidneys as I face my typewriter. But I am not alone. Today, in a self-conscious explosion of intimate talking and writing, many young women are re-educating themselves with new negative formulas about their relationships with men. And one of the most interesting formulas many women are parsing out is how hard it is to give and accept love within a marriage when they feel jealous of their husbands' worldly success. Instead many have decided, as does the heroine of this excellent new novel, to be lonely, self-reliant adults rather than protected child-wives . . .

"The heroine of the book gives a standard, pretend-tough speech to men who fall in love with her. 'Listen, I was married for twelve years and thanks a lot but no thanks. I can't help it, I'm just emotionally claustrophobic and I hope you'll understand. If I wanted a man around all the time to make me miserable I had the best there was so when I ask you to

go please go, because I can't stand feeling guilt and besides,
I'm working on a screenplay.' "

I ended my review with a burst of energy. I was embarrassed to be writing so personally, but I had to. "Two
weeks before I got married in 1964, I flipped through the
pages of some women's magazines in my family doctor's office,
looking for reassurance that this fearful step was the right
one. One fiction story told of a young mother waking up feeling suddenly blue about her limited life. She wishes she were
still being courted by men, the major source of gratification
she learned to manipulate as a teen-ager. Her problems of the
day are solved when she pushes a baby carriage into an old
beau, and after talking to him is exhilarated by the knowledge
that her sometimes absentminded and tired husband is much
less shallow than this fellow who brags about his sexual
conquests and his artistic inability to hold a job.

"This article exemplified the way that women I knew
then wrote and talked about each other's expectations and
roles. At the time I didn't know who I wanted to grow up to
be. As it turns out, I am much closer to Phyllis Raphael's
heroine, and am trying to learn, as are many of my contempo-
raries, to like myself in this role."

I am proud of this review. I think the ease with which
I wrote it and even the ideas come from writing day after
day in this diary. One thing is for sure, it was great to write
something I care about without my *Newsweek* editor waiting
to cross out every word.

June 21

The point is not to feel bad. News travels along my
corridor at work like soap particles in a basin of dishwater.
Everybody finds out everything. They all know I'm slowly

being defeated. Each Friday night it becomes harder and harder to write my few paragraphs. When he edits my copy, I feel like *I'm* being crossed out. I feel like I struggle like crazy to find a defensive position to shield myself, and then get kicked in the stomach anyway.

Lynn called me into her office today. She'd been reading the copies of the stories I'd written last week before and after my editor rewrote them. "Listen," she was running her forefinger slowly under each word as she beckoned to me with her other hand. "I was noticing his corrections on your pieces. He seems to be correcting against modifying and participial phrases. Look." Sure enough, he'd rewritten most of my paragraphs to cancel out all such phrases. I sighed with relief, but it came out more like a groan. Maybe there is some way to turn this mess around.

June 24

It's 11:30 P.M. and I spent the hours on this Friday night consulting with Lynn about how best to write my story of the week about a suit against a government-supported broadcasting station. She came in to say good-night at 9:30, just as I was dramatically tearing up my third version. "Hey, that looks drastic," she said, grabbing the two halves of paper out of my hands. Soon she was sitting at Jim's empty desk and making notes and chewing on her pencil. She waved away my protests. "Shush, I'm trying to think."

While she was working, I sat hunched in my corset, wondering if it wasn't holding me up, whether I'd sag across my desk with exhaustion. "Y'know, Lynn," I burst out, "when I was hired they promised me I could write color stories, features. I can't write these tight news stories. Do you think I should protest?" She stopped moving her pencil. "It's sort

of like those television quiz shows," she said sorrowfully. "If
they want you out and they know your weaknesses, they keep
throwing questions at you that you can't answer. He knows
you have trouble with these stories. You won't get anywhere
complaining to him about them. He's choosing to trip you
up." "Why?" I ask Lynn.

"He probably feels it's his prerogative as a new editor.
We're all getting tested. But since you're the newest, least
experienced person here, he's pushing you hardest."

"Maybe he wants to pick his own recruit. He doesn't
have to train Walter's protégée."

After Lynn finished with my piece, she explained to me
why she had chosen a terse, factual lead sentence. I thanked
her, retyped it, and came home.

I come home alone lately. Somehow all the pressure at
work has taken away my interest in being with men. If I am
feeling so self-hating about my work life, no man is going
to lift the murderous mood I'm in. I am seeing a few people
but they are irritated with my depression over work. Hugh,
a morose poet, is contemptuous of my anxiety. Two nights
ago as I worried what Friday-night writing would bring, he
twisted in his chair in the Japanese restaurant with anger.
"Susan, do you think you're a good writer or not?"

I was pleased that he was finally discussing it with me.
I'd been complaining for about a half hour. "Well, sometimes,
when I write things I really care about like that *Voice* review;
sometimes I think I am good. But then I haven't heard from
the *Voice* about it, so maybe they didn't like it."

He looked furious. "Listen to yourself. *They* didn't like
it. Who cares if other people are shitting on you? If you think
you're good, that's it. So some editor is playing power politics
to get rid of you. Do you really want to write those double-
crostics every week? It doesn't matter what I say, you have
to be convinced. You have to approve of yourself. Why is it

so important to you that this editor likes you. You don't like him or his corrections on your articles, right?"

I peered at Hugh while he picked at his raw tuna fish with his chopsticks. I was looking at him like a punched up fighter who is trying to hear his manager telling him that this isn't his last fight or the crucial one. "Yes, I think you have a point," I answered, putting down my chopsticks. "It's just hard not to feel crappy." He didn't answer, still contemptuous of my anxiety. But I didn't tell him that a poet can afford to wait for the ages to acclaim him. A journalist is writing for people here and now.

He really lost his temper later, when I got sadder after seeing Paul leaving the building next door with Emily. I recognized him by some sixth sense beyond the visual clues of his rolling walk and his bushy hair. Hugh and I were getting out of a cab to go into my building when I grabbed his elbow and said, "Oh, no." I started to cry, and Hugh said dourly, "It means you're still in love." Then I began feeling sorrier than ever for myself, at the age of thirty, crying in my apartment lobby to one man about another. So I stopped, and I told Hugh haughtily, "If you've loved somebody, doesn't part of you always love him?"

June 25

Seeing Paul carried my thoughts back to places I thought I'd forgotten. It's as though that feeling of love I once had was a limb that aches even after amputation. How can I trust both myself and somebody else to love again when I feel so disappointed? Maybe I never will. I have survived. It's true that I can take care of myself. I am the last in line of responsibility for myself. I can now eat protein in the morning, pay

my doctor's bills, balance my checkbook. My job trouble at
Newsweek scares me, but I'm not incapacitated. I'm fighting
back.

June 27

As though she were reading my mind, Alice showed me
a poem yesterday called "Rescue the Dead," by David Igna-
tow, that I'm going to copy part of into this diary.

> . . . To love is to be led away
> into a forest where the secret grave
> is dug, singing, praising the darkness
> under the trees
> *   *   *   *   *   *
> To live is to sign your name
> is to ignore the dead,
> is to carry a wallet
> and shake hands . . .

JULY

July 1

Last night, over a year after my separation, I slept with Carl, one of my husband's oldest friends. I remember our first meeting ten years ago, when I felt myself go up six degrees of happiness in response to his happy giggle, and the laugh crinkles around his eyes. We hadn't seen each other for a year before this week, and out of nowhere I began telling him how amazing it was to have slept with one man until I was twenty-nine, thinking that this was my life, and now finding myself in an era of sexual freedom that I never dreamed I could or would want to take part in. He was a little startled, and so was I. I had forgotten that I had all these options now. Somehow the worry about my work at *Newsweek* made me forget that I could take pleasure in liking a man and thinking about having sex with him. When are my reflexes for pleasing myself going to become as quick as my feelings of worthlessness? Part of my current mood must be based on the fact that the *Voice* printed my review this week. Work dictates my mood. Carl had been lying on my living room rug with his eyes closed and his right leg crossed over his knee. As the hours wore on, we noticed a man in a single lighted window across from my apartment eat a midnight snack. And as we watched, Carl tucked his chin in his elbow and leaned against the couch I was lying on. For about fifteen minutes, I resisted the impulse to stroke his hair. Finally he asked me what I was thinking about. I said, "What are *you* thinking about?" "Sleeping with you," he replied. And I almost cried, my feelings were a mixture of affection and lust and exhaustion. It was strange to stroke his hair, after six years of intimate but not sexual friendship. Yet I really liked mixing our old friendship with sex.

July 20

Carl is gone after three weeks. He will probably live with a fellow math teacher in California this year, a woman I have admired for her brains. And I am alone again. Or am I? I keep thinking about Jill Johnston and wondering if her appeal for me hasn't been in part that she helped me confront some of my own resentments toward men and masculine roles. I am really in pain now that Carl has left and I resent him for leaving. But I now know that the pain and the resentment will last two or three days. Maybe that's the best I can do right now— watch my reactions and wait for the bad ones to diminish. I have a growing knowledge that the loss of any lover, friend, job, money, won't tear me apart. If I do fall apart only a small percentage of me will disintegrate, and then I know I will put myself together. I feel tougher.

Jill says heterosexual women recognize that men hurt them, that men have the power to make women feel second-class. But if women know all this, she asks, why do women still give men their primary sexual energy, and define themselves as failures unless they have a man? An interesting question for me right now. My women friends remain constant;

whereas the ego-gratifying and sexually exciting highs I get from men are impermanent and hurt like hell when they dissipate. I am less responsive to men's advances than I was when Paul and I first broke up. I don't want sexual encounters that mean nothing. The act of making love always hurts somewhere when you realize the gestures of affection aren't authentic. I'd rather be alone. I have proved I can break the old rules. Now I'd like to define some new ones. I have more consistent and realistic expectations of women than I do of men whom I have had sex with. I have fewer fantasies about them. They cannot disappoint me in the same intense ways. Maybe this feminist thing is really a revolution of "limiting" our expectations of what men can do for us, while expanding our expectations of what we can do for ourselves.

I don't perceive women friends as possessions, or as people whose feelings toward me can plunge me into rejected despair. It's not that they are better people. I simply allow them to be themselves.

July 21

It's true—while I am at a loss to define how I want to be with a man, I feel sure of my friendships with women. Last night I went to visit a married couple I know. He is the king of their castle. He chose the meat she cooked for dinner, and grandly points his finger at his favorite fabric sample for the couch. She is the supportive sidekick. I spent one evening talking to her alone while she lovingly sprayed and wiped imaginary fingerprints off the glass framing the thirty very good pictures he's painted that are the main decor of their apartment. Last night, I chatted over coffee with them for an hour. Then I got so angry at him for hogging the show that I stopped talking and left early. Since I knew I'd never have the nerve to tell either of them why I was angry, I got out. As strong an expression of my anger as I'm capable of now.

It's true. Men in their traditional roles as dominant creatures gall me. But my answer to Jill Johnston—I sometimes yearn to be with a man. I'm sure there are men who are willing to be equals. Most important, I have to learn that men don't have to be bigger and better at everything. When I remember my hours of agonized shame as a teen-ager, believing I was too tall to be with most men, I am irritated. I am not yet to the point where I am proud to be tall. I slouch because small hands, small feet, and soft, graceful, tiny gestures defined femininity for me for years. But I am not embarrassed about being taller than any man and the day is coming when I'll be as proud of my height as any sunburned 6′ 3″ male Texan.

AUGUST

August 1

Last night at 8:00 P.M. I angrily told my editor that my most recent piece (written mostly by Lynn) hadn't needed his rewriting. I was scared, but I was emboldened since I was secretly defending Lynn's writing as well as my own.

"If you don't like the way things are run around here . . ." and he was looking at the backs of his hands pressed against the edge of his desk. Then he rose quickly and closed the door. My heart was beating frantically. "You are a decent writer, Susan," he said with a jocular note in his voice. "That piece in the *Voice* on divorce was good. But it wasn't *Newsweek* style." Here, despite his complimentary words, I heard the disapproval. "And frankly, Susan, I'm not sure we all wouldn't be better off if you stopped writing for us."

"I think you're right," I found myself saying. But then my voice stopped. I knew if I continued speaking, I would cry in front of him. So I stood while he rambled on about how hard he'd tried to train me, how much time he'd devoted to me to the detriment of his other writers.

"I disagree with you," I managed to say. "I don't think you helped me at all." Then I saw that his chin was shaking in addition to the pencil-tapping and foot-bouncing he was doing. He stood behind his huge desk, his face red. "Well, then there's nothing to say," he said, starting to walk toward the door. "So this is hard on you too," I mumbled, realizing that he was not just the enemy. "The day it becomes easy, I'll hang up my corporate collar," he said distantly.

So I rushed to my office to cry. Later, Ann, a researcher, hugged me when I told her my news in a quavery voice. "Don't worry, you're better off out of here. You'll see soon enough," she kept saying. Another woman came in to report that the top brass were furious. It seems that my editor had fallen into our conversation without much advance planning. And his bosses were scared that the women were going to revolt.

Then a third woman slid past them into my office. She was the *Newsweek* union representative and she urged me to consider a suit. The support felt good. But I started crying again and said. "Well, the only thing I'll miss about this goddam place is all of you." "Listen," one woman said, "we're not going to lose track of you."

I have decided that I should at least act confident. So I am coming to work every day until my two weeks are up. Lynn keeps telling me, "Nobody takes being fired from *Newsweek* as a black mark against your writing ability, believe me." Well, I am trying to believe her. I am also proud of the fact that I have saved about $5,000 in the past eight months, ever since I began feeling nervous about the new editor. So I can subsidize myself while I try free-lance writing for a year.

Last night I called Paul and asked if I could borrow some money from him over the next few months. It was a contradictory bid for affection. "I have nobody else to ask, Paul," I said in a menacing voice. I wondered if he wondered why I didn't sound apologetic. "I've lost my job and I'm not sure what I'll earn free-lancing." He immediately started quizzing me. "Well, umm, wait a minute, how much do you think you'd need?" And in a flash I was angry with him, because he wasn't sure he could be generous. "I don't know."

I answered truthfully. "About $100 a month, maybe $250." I knew I had to name a higher figure than I wanted. I was also ashamed to be asking for money—as though I were admitting I couldn't cope without him. But I felt helpless. "What?" he exploded. "Paul, there's no one else I could ask. I worked while you were in graduate school. I never asked for anything back for that. Now I am asking you for a loan. I could have asked for alimony," I threatened unconvincingly. "I'll see," he answered, abashed.

August 15

I ignore Paul's hints that we should see each other. I guess I still feel hurt. We shared too much. I can't establish a relationship with him yet that is only superficial. I used to tease that I didn't trust him, that he was a stranger to me, but he is the only person I feel I can ask for money. Last night I called him, wondering why he hadn't called me back about the loan. "Oh, he's right here," Emily said. The sound of her voice still makes me angry. But I swear she still sounds scared of me.

"It's impossible," Paul said. "What?" "I can't afford to give you money." I heard self-pity in his voice. "Anyway I'd probably just be trying to buy your friendship. Emily and I just make do." "What?" I repeated. "What the hell are you talking about? You know that trip to France that you both took." I shocked myself with the bitter tone in my voice. "Well, that was partly my vacation. I worked while you went to graduate school." I didn't want to go to France at all. Why am I saying this? I am lying to him again.

"Maybe, but Emily can't get a good job," he said stubbornly. I had to remember not to shout. "Well, I don't have a job either—for the first time since we got married."

"Okay, okay." He is easily moved by my talk of our past.

"But I can't lend you more than a hundred a month, and not as alimony but as a friend." "That's good, Paul," I answered. "Don't think I won't do the same for you, if you ask me." As I write I am pursing my lips to make sure I don't cry out loud. I chose well, when I chose a husband. I can't picture choosing one again, but I chose a reliable person that time. I stop crying when I think about his basic unwillingness to give me the money.

It's a strange time. I'm scared in much the same way I was when Paul and I split up. But I know more now. I know that there is something about me that is stronger.

I have enormous energy. I wake each morning alert with resolve. I call editors, announcing grandly that I want to write for them. At least once a day, of course, I collapse into self-pity: no more $16,000-a-year job, office, medical insurance, expense account, and daily schedule. But the mood passes when I remember I don't have to face Friday-night editing. Now I can get back to the kind of writing I care about.

I call my friends to tell them with some bravado that I'm no longer at *Newsweek*. I shock some of them by announcing that I was fired. "When did you give notice?" asks an editor. I answer, "I had a fight with my editor and he said get out." Most of my friends are relieved that I'm straightforward. They discuss the deficiencies of group journalism and mass-produced writing. I am telling people to come to my house on Saturday night for a party launching my free-lance career.

August 20

Why do I study the people I report on and write about so much? It makes for better articles, and each has something to show me, I guess. Once, years ago, I became totally absorbed in the works of a Southern writer whose lined, lizard-like face marked him as a man who'd dared a full emotional life. Rewarded by society as an artist, he learned to describe his emotional hunches in prose and poetry and to live by them. A year and a half ago, James Taylor's music hit me like a quick memory of a dream. So I badgered the *Times* to let me write a profile of him, an assignment I'd originally turned down. I believe that writing, especially profiles, saved me. I watched these people and I learned the value of a life enriched by work that one truly loves. I also learned that failure to gain approval had rarely stopped these people.

Before I started looking at other lives, I was afraid to have opinions, afraid to admit the imperfections in my own life. When I confronted people who demand the right to understand and express their feelings or to create from their private perceptions, they became my primers on how to live.

In my article I described the Southern writer's hand movements as he spoke of a woman facing death. First he smacked his chest with both hands and then reached toward the face of a student. I wrote about him looking out of the corner of his eye at his playwriting students and worrying whether he should confide his dread about waking up in the morning to face writing his novel. And I watched James Taylor pick out new love songs on his guitar, while he stared into the corner of his motel room like a blind person with only one sense developed. If he hadn't had this outlet, he told me, he would be purely insane, impacted. Insanity versus self-expression. Is that simplistic? I don't know. But I feel like that sometimes about my own work.

I began to believe that I too had something to express, some vision of reality had been growing inside me. When I confided my perceptions to Paul, he was often embarrassed or gently corrective, so I stopped trying. Writing articles and my diary then became my outlet. As an expert on a novelist I could write about the autobiographical fragments of his poetry, his sadness and joy over his advancing age, and his love of his young children. Slowly I began to believe that I had an eye for reality, and the world took form for me as I forced myself to confide my judgments and hunches about people's motives and feelings to my typewriter. Journalism was for me a second chance at life. A chance to inhale and exhale the world. And to wonder finally about the beginning, the achievement, and the end of my own life.

August 23

The party was a success. I started organizing it a few days ago. It was easier than giving parties with Paul. He refused to let me start buying ice and arranging napkins and punch glasses until a few hours before the party began. I hated the last-minute rush. I know people were having a good time last night. I overheard Judith and Lynn discussing how *Newsweek* has been good for me, but it was time I started writing about subjects that I cared about. I thought about John Schwartz several times as I looked over the guests—feeling sorry that I hadn't invited him. We've had a few warm telephone conversations recently. Now that I'm not falling apart, we will be able to be friends. I don't feel I need him, so I can enjoy him. We are emotional equals. He's a nervous, fearful person—somewhat like me—and we can take turns soothing each other.

It was the first time Lynn and her husband had come to my apartment. We can be friends outside *Newsweek*. I was so proud that I gave the party on my own. Everyone in the living room was someone that I like. I am slowly reorganizing my life. Instead of loving one person I am trying to invest my affection in several good people. And in my work. And hopefully in myself.

Marriage as a necessity of my life is gone, although sometimes I want to scream for someone like Paul to love me. I felt this more in the first months after Paul left: I hated John Schwartz because he wouldn't comfort me endlessly. I still lapse into fragments of the old fantasy at odd moments and then feel elated as I think, "Aah, he'll be the one to take care of me." Then reality intrudes fast, and I discover that Carl, for instance, would rather worry about finding the perfect double-knit suit to wear at his lectures or about pure mathematics than about my money woes, and that I'd rather take care of my own problems my own way or talk to my friend Lynn instead of his physicist friend, Allen. The fantasy fades and then we must decide if we want to become friends and not lifesavers.

But, most important, I can sit at my typewriter, ask friends out to dinner, telephone editors to suggest assignments, and take my clothing to the cleaners on schedule. I guess I am getting independent. I don't desperately need to see myself as part of a couple at parties or when I'm alone. I don't even need right now to be "dating" a man or sleeping with anyone.

When I used to catch glimpses of Paul and me—in dark mirrors in entrance foyers at a party or in our bathroom mirror with me looking over his shoulder while he shaved, I used to be struck by how much handsomer each of our faces looked together. The other day I saw my reflection in a jewelry-store window while I was staring at a wristwatch I might buy (I am tired of having to ask other people for the time) and I didn't recognize my reflection for a second. Then I looked closely and I liked the fact that my shoulders seem higher than they've been for a while. And I liked the fact that I was seeing myself alone and enjoying the moment.

Breaking up a marriage is a painful ritual, harder, I think, than starting a marriage. Both steps mean risking a large chunk of your identity. When I was younger I believed adults knew why they did such things. Now I know it will take me years to understand even a little of what happened.

And my understanding will always be partly defensive or revisionist. But the important thing is that I have survived and
probably grown. Last night as I put the bag of trash out my
back door after the party, I suddenly thought: I am halfway
through my life, and I am learning to do most things better
than I ever did before.